LIFE
IN
GAMBIA

The Smiling Coast of Africa

Makonnen Sankofa

Published in London, United Kingdom by
Independent Publishing Network

ISBN: 9781800493216

DEDICATION

This book is dedicated to the lovely people of Gambia who welcomed me with open arms and made my experiences in Gambia memorable, emotional and pleasurable.

CONTENTS

INTRODUCTION

Officially named Republic of the Gambia, the country is also commonly known as The Gambia or Gambia. It is a small country in West Africa that is situated by the coast of the Atlantic Ocean. Gambia is an English-speaking country, which has a population of around 2.5 million people. Gambia is known globally as the home of Kunta Kinte. In Alex Haley's novel and television series *Roots*, the main character Kunta Kinte is a Gambian from the village of Juffureh. Like hundreds of thousands of other Gambians, Kunta Kinte was captured, enslaved, and transported from Gambia to the USA.

Since the arrival of the Portuguese in the 15th century, several European countries have occupied settlements and trading posts along the Gambia River. What started off as trading goods, gradually turned into the trade of human beings as part of the transatlantic slave trade. Gambians were captured in areas along the Gambia River. Men, women and children were kidnapped and sold off into slavery. Many of the Gambians sold off into slavery, were from rival tribes of other Gambians and prisoners of war. James Island (renamed Kunta Kinte Island) was one of the places where enslaved Gambians were kept in awful conditions before being transported to countries in the Americas on ships.

In 1807, slave trading was outlawed by the British Empire. Between 1821-1965, Gambia was an official colony of Britain. Gambia gained independence on 18 February, 1965. Gambia's first president Dawda Jawara, ruled until Yahya Jammeh seized power in a coup in 1994. Adama Barrow became Gambia's third president in January 2017, after defeating Jammeh in the elections that took place during December 2016. Gambia has had some political instability and corruption in the past. However, Gambia is very peaceful country with a low crime rate.

Gambia's friendly people, hot weather, lovely beaches, and close proximity to Europe make it an ideal tourist destination for people living in Europe to travel to. In terms of moving from the West to live in Gambia, some people are attracted to moving to Gambia because the cost of living, accommodation, and transport is cheaper in Gambia compared to countries in the West.

This book is split up into three sections about my time spent in Gambia. In Part 1, you will get an insight into my first trip to Gambia. This includes how I felt arriving in Africa for the first time, my interactions with the staff at the hotel, my night out in the popular Senegambia strip, my experience of going to the famous Kunta Kinte Island, how I was treated by the local Gambian people, and my trips to the local markets.

In Part 2, it's about my second time in Gambia. I highlight the pros and cons of doing business in Gambia and I also give suggestions of business opportunities that may be successful in Gambia. Later on in Part 2, you will find out how I spent my time with the native Gambians. As you discover more about my journey, you will get insight into what everyday life is like for the *average Gambian*.

In Part 3, it's about my six months stay in Gambia. I had a very eventful time on my third visit to Gambia. I went to a few traditional Gambian naming ceremonies, experienced a Gambian wedding, mingled with influential Gambians, made plenty of friends, delivered lectures in schools, and worked with Juliet Ryan on the popular Blaxit YouTube channel which had thousands of subscribers worldwide. Other things I cover in Part 3, is how living in Gambia improved my health, societal values and the culture in Gambia, the gap between the rich and poor, how safe Gambia is to live in, the simplicity of getting procedures done in Gambia (such as extending my stay in the country), the campaign for automatic citizenship for descendants of enslaved Africans returning home, the effect of Thomas Cook going out of business on tourism in Gambia, and how I felt about moving back to England after spending six months outside the country.

The purpose of writing this book about Gambia is to give people *first-hand* information about the country, which is primarily based on my experiences of being in Gambia and what I learned whilst I was there. This book provides valuable information on a wide variety of topics. This book is ideal for anyone wishing to visit or move to Gambia, particularly people of African heritage in the diaspora. Anyone with a general interest in Gambia, will also benefit by reading this book.

PART 1: MY FIRST VISIT TO GAMBIA

CHAPTER 1

My first journey to Gambia was in December, 2018. As a Pan-Africanist and Rastafarian, my goal is to live in Africa permanently. For several years, I have been a community activist focused on black liberation. It's important that we have a connection to Africa as black people because that's our ancestral homeland. For those of us in the diaspora that are descendants of enslaved Africans, our ancestors were stripped off their culture and identity during slavery. Therefore, we have a gap that is missing inside us. We have been disconnected from our motherland; this is like a child being raised without a mother and put in someone else's care.

My first time visiting Africa was in 2018. My

friend Justin Muhammad invited me to go with him to Gambia. Justin was already planning to go Gambia with his friend Lady M. Justin's friend has been travelling to Gambia for years and she is married to a Gambian. Justin hadn't been to Gambia before we went on that trip. But he had already travelled to other countries in Africa.

We arrived at Banjul International Airport on Monday 10 December, 2018. The plane journey was 6 hours 30 minutes from London Gatwick to Banjul International Airport. When I got off the plane, I felt the heat straight away. It was a typical hot and sunny day in Gambia. As I walked down the steps of the plane, it was at that point that I thought to myself that many of my ancestors who had been taken away from Africa 400 years ago, never had the chance to return to their homeland. Therefore, I had a feeling of satisfaction and gratitude within myself to be in Africa. My ancestors were able to return to Africa through my body and spirit. I honour my ancestors who experienced so much inhumane treatment during the transatlantic slave trade between the 16th and 19th centuries, when over twelve million Africans were captured and transported from Africa and taken to the Americas, where they were forced into a life of slavery.

After Justin and I passed immigration and

picked up our luggage, we joined Lady M and the other people that came with Lady M to Gambia. Before we went on this trip to Gambia, Justin and I hadn't met the other people who came to Gambia with Lady M. Everyone kept together at the airport because the group of us were all going to the same hotel. There were nine of us in total (seven adults, two children). At the airport, we were greeted by Lady M's husband Kebba and Lady M's friend Adama. Like Kebba, Adama is also a Gambian. Both of them drove us to Badala Park Hotel in Kotu, where we stayed during the holiday.

When we got to the hotel, we went to the reception and checked into our rooms. The hotel caretaker, Bounty, carried my luggage and showed me into my room. I didn't like my room because it was on the ground floor, near the front door which was wide open. I was worried that mosquitoes, insects, and other creatures would come into my room because the building door on the ground floor was open.

Malaria is prevalent in Gambia. I talked to Bounty about how to prevent myself from getting malaria and about the likelihood of me getting bitten by a mosquito and becoming infected with malaria. Bounty put my mind at ease about malaria by what he told me. He emphasised to me that not every mosquito bite will give a person malaria. He also told me that malaria was less prevalent at that particularly time of year (dry season). Bounty recommended that I buy a mosquito killer spray to use in my room before bedtime, to keep mosquitos away during the night.

Bounty and I had a conversation about Pan-Africanism. We also spoke about the relevance of my journey to Africa as someone of African heritage born and raised in the diaspora. I remember when Bounty said to me, "You're a black man, this (Africa) is your home." I was happy to be welcomed to Gambia in the way Bounty embraced me. After our conversation, Bounty and I went to the local shop to get the mosquito killer spray. Whilst I was walking on the street, I felt so happy to be in Gambia. The air was fresh and the area near the hotel looked beautiful.

On the way back to the hotel from the mini mart, I noticed one of the local vendors had some hats on display. There was a Rastafarian hat with the colours red, gold and green. I bought the hat from the street vendor, whose name is Sailou. I didn't have enough Gambian dalasi left on me after coming back from the mini mart. Therefore, I gave Sailou £5 and told him to get the money changed at the Western Union across the road.

When Bounty and I got back to the hotel, I saw Justin in the reception talking to the hotel manager. Justin wasn't happy with his room, so he arranged to get his room swapped. Fortunately, I was also able to get my room swapped. Shortly after we went into our new rooms, Justin had a nap because he was tired as a result of all the travelling from England to the hotel in Gambia. Whilst Justin was sleeping in his room, I went outside of my room and took a walk around the hotel complex. There was a swimming pool, bar/restaurant, a stage for entertainment, and another area designated for breakfast meals.

There was a Gambian man with a small stand from which he was selling books at the hotel. I understood why he was selling books because a lot of people like to read a book during their leisure time on holiday. But I found it strange being in an African country and seeing the vendor selling books by only white authors. He didn't have any books by black authors about Gambia, African history, African culture, or contemporary books about Africa. At that time, I was still in the process of writing my first book *The Rise of Rastafari: Resistance, Redemption & Repatriation*. If my book was available at that time, I would have spoken to the vendor about selling copies of it.

As I was walking around the hotel complex, I started to feel hungry. I saw a young man standing around who looked like hotel staff. He was actually one of the hotel volunteers. His nickname is Happy. We spoke briefly and then we went out of the hotel to get something to eat.

Happy took me to a local Gambian-owned restaurant. At the restaurant, they served a mixture of traditional Gambian foods and fast food such as pizza, burgers and chips. I had a pizza and it tasted delicious. I shared some slices with Happy. After we left the restaurant, we went to a local shop that I wanted to go in and then we made our way back to the hotel. On the way back to the hotel, it was very dark. There were no street lights. The main source of light came from the lights of the cars that were driving by. I had to be very careful when walking. Therefore, we decided to get one of the cabs that were driving past to take us back to the hotel.

When we got back to the hotel, Happy introduced me to some of the staff who worked at the hotel. They were young males that looked between 20-30 years old. I was 28 when I visited Gambia. It was good to be with a group of young Gambians within the same age group as me. The guys had either finished work or they were off-duty. Happy and I sat down and joined them. There were six of us altogether. We drank some green tea, which is called "attire" by the native Gambians. In Gambia, it is common for people to drink green tea every day. Sometimes people drink green tea several times throughout the day. I remember when Happy was making green tea, I was surprised when I saw how much sugar he was using to mix the drink. Once I tasted the green tea, I could definitely taste the sweetness of the sugar in the drink.

I was curious and intrigued to find out what life was like for the young men as native Gambians. Vice versa, they were interested to hear about my experience of living in England. We had a good discussion about the realities of living in different parts of the world. One of the guys asked me, "How does it feel to be home in Africa?". We also spoke about Rastafari and reggae. The guys love reggae music like me. We were talking about reggae artists and they mentioned the names of the reggae singers that had been to Gambia. Then, one of the guys put on reggae music from his phone.

Shortly after that, one of them brought over some food in a big bowl. Gambians normally eat together from a large bowl. Some Gambians use their hands to eat food, others use a spoon. They offered me a spoon. I took the spoon and had a little bit of the food. I wasn't hungry because I had eaten a large pizza earlier. However, I wanted to experience the taste of Gambian food. Also, I thought out of courtesy I would try some of the food.

In Gambia, it is good manners to eat food that is offered to you. I wasn't pressured to eat the food. Happy mentioned to me that if I didn't want to eat the food or that if I felt uncomfortable about eating the food, I should not bother eating it. The food was rice mixed with some sauce. There was a piece of meat on top of the rice in the centre of the bowl. There were also some vegetables. Traditionally in a Gambian family household, the piece of meat on top of the rice in the centre is normally left for the male head of the household to eat.

After the meal, Happy and I separated from the group and we went to the hotel bar to get drinks. When we got there, I saw Justin. He was re-energised after his nap. Justin and I went to the reception, so Justin could speak to the hotel manager about something. After that, Justin and I decided to head out and do a bit of exploring. We went to Senegambia, which is the most popular tourist area in Gambia.

The Senegambia strip has a variety of bars, restaurants and nightclubs. Justin and I went into one of the bars/restaurants. I enjoyed the live band performing reggae music. They were singing classic reggae songs such as "Stir It Up" by Bob Marley. Whilst at the venue watching the band, I turned my head and I saw a beautiful young lady behind me. I was attracted to her pretty face, nice figure, and lovely long hair. Her skin complexion is light brown, like my skin colour. I remember thinking to myself at the time, this girl looks like a supermodel. Shortly after I saw her, Justin and I left the venue because it was closing time there.

We went to another bar/restaurant across the road. A live band was also playing in that bar/restaurant. As Justin and I were sitting down watching the band perform, the woman I saw from the previous venue came into the bar/restaurant by herself. She went to the bar to order a drink and then she sat down at one of the tables. I thought to myself, I've got to approach her. I glanced over to look at her and she was looking back at me. So, I signaled to her to come over to me.

The lady came over and we started talking. She told me her name but I am going to keep her name anonymous. I will refer to her in this book as Ayesha. She explained to me that she is from Guinea and that she moved to Gambia years ago because she had a family member or close friend in Gambia. Then, she explained to me that she met her ex-husband in Gambia and they had a business together. After she broke up with her ex-husband, she left the country but she came back in hope there would be better opportunities for her in Gambia compared to her home country Guinea. Ayesha told me she was in her early 30s.

During the conversation, Ayesha mentioned that there was a nightclub around the corner which would be a good place for us to go to. So, we went to the nightclub. When we got there, we got some drinks and then Ayesha and I started dancing to the dancehall and reggae music that the DJ was playing. After we left the club, Ayesha drove Justin and I back to the hotel in her luxury car.

When we got back to the hotel, we said goodnight to my friend Justin. Then, Ayesha and I went into my room. We had a conversation about some of our personal experiences. I think we connected well. But there was something at the back of my mind thinking, what's this girl's motive? Is she after my money? Will I wake up in the morning and discover that she has stolen some of my stuff? I thought in that way because I had just met her that night, it was my first time on holiday in Gambia, and I hadn't had any experience with women in Gambia before that point.

I have heard and read about incidents when men have gone abroad on holiday and been conned by women. This can happen in different ways. Sometimes, a man sleeps with a woman overnight. The next day, the man wakes up, the woman is gone, and the man's finds out that his stuff has been stolen. I'm someone who tends to be cautious of things in general, so I did have my *guard up* with Ayesha. But I realised that I would have to take responsibility for whatever happened, whether it be good or bad because I was the one who approached her and I was the one who invited her back to my hotel room.

Ayesha and I slept together overnight and she left the hotel the following morning. I wasn't sure whether I was going to arrange to see Ayesha again because I was on holiday and I wanted to spend time exploring Gambia. I was thinking that I had a good time with her the previous night but I should just leave it at that. Ayesha called me on WhatsApp when she got home. She was in bed and about to go back to sleep. She said she wanted to see me later on, I agreed to see her but I was still skeptical about her at that point.

I went downstairs to get some water and I met up with Justin. We didn't eat the hotel breakfast that morning, so we were both hungry. Justin's friends Mali and Angel (married couple) owned a Jamaican restaurant which was a 10 minutes walk from the hotel where Justin and I stayed at. Mali and Angel's restaurant was called Mosiah's. Both Justin and I are of Caribbean heritage and we're used to eating Jamaican food. Therefore, it made sense for us to go to Mosiah's and have some of the same types of food were used to eating. Us visiting Mosiah's also gave Justin time to catch up with Mali and Angel.

When we got to Mosiah's, it was the first-time I met Mali and Angel. Mali and I have a lot of mutual friends due to our activism within black communities in England. A few weeks before going to Gambia, Justin introduced me to Angel's son and Mali's stepson, who lives in England. Mali and Angel named their restaurant Mosiah's in honour of the great Pan-African activist, Marcus Mosiah Garvey. At Mosiah's, the restaurant was decorated in Marcus Garvey's Pan-African colours of red, black and green. The food I ate at Mosiah's was very nice. I had jerk chicken with rice and peas. Justin and I were sitting upstairs, overlooking a nice view of the surrounding area and the sea. Mali and Angel joined us at the table and we had a good conversation with them. (Mali and Angel have moved location of their restaurant to Kololi. Their new restaurant is called Mo2, which is a short abbreviation of Mosiah's 2.)

Later that evening, Ayesha gave me a call and told me she was coming to the hotel to see me. We went out to a couple of the nightclubs in Senegambia. Then, we went back to the hotel and she stayed overnight with me. Throughout my holiday, Ayesha and I spent a lot of time together and we got to know each other better as time went on. What I liked about Ayesha was that besides her good looks, she was well mannered and very respectful to me and people in general.

One of the places Ayesha and I went to was Serrekunda Market. I remember that the place was huge and that there was a wide variety of shops both inside the market building and outside on the streets. The marketplace was vibrant; there was a hustle and bustle type of atmosphere. Serrekunda Market is one of the main places Gambians go to get food, clothes, electronics, and household items. Ayesha and I also went to Banjul Market but I preferred Serrekunda Market because there was a better range of products there.

In one of the shops at Banjul Market, Ayesha wanted to buy a top which had the city name Paris written on the front of the t-shirt and beneath the writing there was a picture of the Eiffel Tower. I thought it was strange that an

African woman would want to wear a top like that because Ayesha had never been to France and France is the country which invaded Guinea (her native country) and made Guinea a French colony during the scramble for Africa. As a conscious black man and a proud African, this was something I didn't like and I voiced my opinion about this to Ayesha. In my mind, her wearing that Paris top would be her flaunting her former coloniser. After speaking with me, Ayesha bought another top from the shop.

CHAPTER 2

On Thursday that week, I went on a trip to Juffureh and its neighbouring village Albreda. I travelled there along with Justin, Lady M, and the other people who came to Gambia with Lady M. We left the hotel early in the morning. Adama and Kebba droves us to Banjul Port. From Banjul, we got on a boat that took us to Juffureh. The village of Juffureh is famous because of Alex Haley's television series *Roots*. In the series, it highlights the life of Kunta Kinte and his descendants.

According to Alex Haley, Kunta Kinte was a real-life person who was captured in Juffureh and enslaved. After he was captured in Juffureh, he was taken to a small island called James Island (renamed Kunta Kinte island). Kunta Kinte was kept on that island until he was transported to the USA. During the transatlantic slave trade, there were millions of Africans like Kunta Kinte who were transported from Gambia and other parts of West Africa to the Americas. But this wasn't the end of their *misery*. For the enslaved Africans who arrived in the Americas, their lives continued to be a *living hell*.

When thinking about what happened during the transatlantic slave trade, it's despicable how one group of people treated another group of people so brutal. It's distressing to think how evil human beings can be towards their fellow men and women. It's like the people that enslaved the other people didn't have a *soul*. The transatlantic slave trade was a crime against humanity that has left a traumatic legacy on the descendants of those who were enslaved, which still exists today. The transatlantic slave trade has also contributed to shaping a societal structure where you have inequalities in how people are treated in society because of people's racial background.

During slavery, the people enslaving other humans were white Europeans and the enslaved were black Africans. Although slavery was abolished in the Americas over 130 years ago, societies have maintained a racist hierarchy where white people are treated better than black people or mixed people because the colour of their skin. The horrible legacy of the transatlantic slave trade has also created a massive divide in wealth and economic power between black and white people. The privilege white society got rich off slavery by forcing the enslaved Africans to work for free on plantations to extract raw materials and produce goods (such as cotton, sugar, rum, tobacco) that the slave owners would sell to make lots of money. When slavery was eventually abolished in the Caribbean, the British government paid £20 million (around £17 billion as of 2015) in compensation to the slave owners for their projected financial loss as a result of freeing the slaves.

The money made by slave owners and the money given to them in compensation has trickled down to their descendants through inheritance of generational wealth. This has been through money, businesses, property, land, and possessions. However, the enslaved Africans were freed without any compensation given to them. Therefore, they had no land, no money, no food, and no homes. They had to start from scratch. In the USA, various laws were put in place after slavery to deprive black people of having rights to acquire land, set up business, vote, or enjoy the same benefits as white people in the society.

In Albreda, we visited the slavery museum. It's a very small museum, so we were only in there for about 20 minutes. On the walls, I saw pictures and texts of information about the transatlantic slave trade. I also saw a section dedicated to people of African heritage from the diaspora that have made a significant impact on black history globally. I remember seeing information on the wall about Martin Luther King Jr. and Bob Marley among others. I was disappointed because of the small size of the museum and the little amount of information that was on display at the museum, especially considering the history of slavery in Gambia. Visiting the museum would have also been a much better experience if we had a guided tour with someone talking about the Gambian history of the transatlantic slave trade.

Across the sea from Juffureh, is the nearby Kunta Kinte island (formerly known as James Island). It takes about five minutes on a boat to get from the village of Juffureh to Kunta Kinte island. I imagined the brutality and indignity of what the enslaved Africans had to endure: from being captured, to being held in dungeons for long periods, to being packed next to each other on slave ships with shackles around their hands and feet and little room to move, people having to urinate and defecate in the same space they were kept in, the indignity of being sold off to strangers in a public auction, being branded with a hot iron as someone's property, the lashes on the plantation given to the enslaved Africans by the slave master or overseer, women raped, children made to watch their dad be raped by another man (buck breaking), mutilation of people's body parts, people being hanged to death, humans being burned alive for rebelling on the plantation and trying to gain their freedom.

There is no amount of money, gold, or anything else that can compensate or undo the physical, mental, and generational damage that the transatlantic slave trade has caused. That horrific legacy has also caused a disconnection between Africans on the continent and the descendants of the enslaved Africans in the diaspora. In Gambia, I noticed that there was a lack of awareness amongst many Gambians regarding how black people in the diaspora (Black British, Caribbean, African Americans) are connected to Africa.

I recall speaking to a Gambian I know. He asked me, "Is Jamaica in Africa?". From his response, it indicated to me that his geography is bad and that he didn't know slaves were taken to Jamaica. On another occasion, I remember speaking with a Gambian and he thought that enslaved Africans were taken from Africa and sent to America and England. He didn't know that millions of enslaved Africans were taken to the Caribbean as well as America but not to England. Over a century after slavery was abolished in the Caribbean, descendants of enslaved Africans immigrated to England during the Windrush era. It's a shame that despite the fact that hundreds of thousands of Gambians were kidnapped, enslaved and transported from Gambia, many Gambians don't have much knowledge about slavery, especially about what happened to the enslaved Gambians after they left Gambia.

There is a big division in society between how black and white people are treated in the West. Most Gambians and also other Africans on the continent are unaware of this. In Gambia, they don't know what racism is and they are unaware about the kind of racism that happens to black people in the diaspora. Part of the reason black people from the diaspora are moving to Africa, is to get away from white people and escape racism. But in the eyes of the local Gambians, black people in the diaspora are like white people because both set of people live in the same country.

Most Gambians regard those of us who were born and raised in the diaspora as Westerners, regardless of our skin colour. Even if you have one or two parents who were born and raised in Gambia or another part of Africa, they will still regard you as a Westerner. Therefore, there is a feeling of limbo by descendants of enslaved Africans. This is because when we are in the West, we are regarded as foreigners and also when we are in Africa, we are regarded as foreigners. I understand to some degree why Gambians regard descendants of enslaved Africans from the diaspora as Westerners because we have been in the diaspora for generations since leaving Africa. And, to some extent black people born and raised in the diaspora are Westerners because we live or have lived most of our lives in the West and have got accustomed to Western culture, languages, values, politics, and way of life.

But I find it strange and inconsistent how most Gambians tend to identify black people based on nationality but they identify other races of people based on heritage. For example, they all regard an Indian as Asian. No matter whether the person was born in Gambia or not. They all see a white man as European, no matter whether the person was born in Gambia or not. However, Gambians refer to black people born in England as English and black people born in America as American.

I have a brown skin complexion, which is similar to many Ethiopians (East Africans) and the San people (Southern Africans). When I was in Gambia, I saw some Gambians who had similar skin complexions to my skin colour. Those people were mainly from the Fulani tribe (also known as Fula). There were also people living in Gambia from other parts of Africa who had similar skin complexions to mine. Some Gambian women had bleached their skin and that made them look lighter than their natural skin tone. But the majority of Gambian men are black or dark brown in skin colour. So, a lot of Gambians thought I'm half black, half white. Some people thought I'm Fulani, or light-skinned but not necessarily mixed. However, many people thought that one of my parents is native Gambian and my other parent is white European.

Over the course of my three stays in Gambia, I was even referred to as a white person (toubab) on a few occasions because my skin colour is brown and not black. It was weird and false being referred to as white because my skin colour is brown. I refer to myself as black because that's the common term used to describe people from dark black skin to light brown skin, whose ethnicity is mainly of African/Caribbean heritage.

Neither of my parents are white. My mum is of black Jamaican heritage and my dad is half black Malawian (South East African) and half Indian. Technically, I am three-quarters black. I had a black upbringing from being raised by my mum and all my family I know are black. My dad who is half black, was even born and raised in Africa. He came to England in his earlier twenties. My mum told me that she initially thought my dad was full black because of his appearance and also because she used to often see him with black people. It wasn't until later on when my dad told her he was half black and half Indian that she was aware he wasn't full black.

One time, my mum showed me a picture of my dad when he was younger. In that picture, my dad had a big Afro. I looked at his hair and his skin complexion; he looked full black. Nowadays, my dad looks mixed black and Indian. He also looks more Somalian compared to how he looked in that picture I saw when he was younger. Although my dad is mixed race, his skin complexion is darker than mine and my mum's skin complexion.

My ethnicity is completely different to a person who is half black, half white. Neither is my skin colour visibly white like Mariah Carey, Jesse Williams or Meghan Markle (who are half black but look white). So, it was strange that on a few occasions I was referred to as white. From speaking to other *brown people* in Gambia (who are from the diaspora), they told me they were also called white by some of the native Gambians. And, some of those other *brown people* are even darker than me. For some crazy reason, in Gambia (like some other parts of Africa), it's common for people of brown skin tones to be called white (regardless of the background of that person's parents). I used to get offended about this but then I realised that people are not trying to insult me, it's just that they have a very ignorant way of thinking.

Ayesha called herself "half-caste" even though both her parents are African. The reason she called herself "half-caste" is because her skin colour is brown and her parents are from two different African countries. Ayesha told me that she identifies herself as African but not black because she only regards people as black if their skin colour is literally black. There are many Gambians (and other Africans) who think like Ayesha and consider people with brown skin tones as a different ethnicity to dark-skinned black people (even if the person's ethnicity is not half-caste). I noticed that the people I came across who were that way inclined with their thinking, also regard people as half-caste if someone has parents of different nationalities. Therefore, if someone's parents are of different races and different nationalities, that person will be regarded as "two-caste" or "double half-caste".

Being viewed as a *half-caste* foreigner (on first impression) in Gambia wasn't necessarily a bad thing because I was welcomed with open arms everywhere I went and I was fully accepted and embraced by the Gambian people. I wasn't discriminated against because of my brown skin colour. Neither was I given any privileges by being a *brown person*. However, I was a bit insecure about my skin colour and I wanted to have darker skin like most of the Gambian men. The reason why I felt like that, is because I didn't want people to look at me as a half-caste person. Ironically, I came across dark-skinned black people who liked my brown skin colour and they wished their skin was the same complexion as mine (particularly women).

Gambians are hospitable and receptive to people from all walks of life and people of all ethnicities. For that reason, Gambia is known as *the smiling coast of Africa*. Gambians are the friendliest people I've met in my life. Every time I went to Gambia, the natives showed me so much love and they took care of me very well. When I went Gambia the first time, I was pleasantly surprised because I wasn't expecting the natives to be so welcoming as they were towards me.

Although I only stayed in Gambia for a week on my first visit, I felt like I was there for twice as long because I had an eventful week. When I got back to England, Ayesha and I stayed in regular communication with each other through WhatsApp. We spoke on the phone most days. I went back to Gambia for Ayesha's birthday in February, 2019. Although I went to see Ayesha for her birthday, I also went to Gambia because I wanted to do more research on business opportunities in the country. Ayesha had some good qualities I liked but I was thinking of breaking up with her because I felt our personalities clashed and we valued different things.

I had already bought my plane ticket to go Gambia before I was thinking of breaking up with Ayesha. Therefore, I thought I would see how it goes with her when I got to Gambia and make a decision what to do with her whilst I was there. But in the back of my mind, I thought it would be best to break up with her. If Ayesha and I broke up before I booked my ticket and didn't go Gambia to see her in February, 2019, I would still have gone back to Gambia. But it would have been a couple of months later, to do exploring of business opportunities in Gambia.

PART 2: MY SECOND VISIT TO GAMBIA

CHAPTER 3

The second time I arrived in Gambia was on 12 February, 2019. After my first trip to Gambia, I was considering setting up a tour company for tourists. So, I did research on the other tour companies in the popular tourist areas during my second time in Gambia. I also went to a few car lots to have a look at some vehicles. Initially, I was interested in getting a small mini bus. However, the prices were expensive. Even the prices for the standard cars were higher than what I thought it would be. And, I didn't like the condition of many of the vehicles I saw.

The reason why the cars were expensive was because the cars had been imported from Europe. Vehicles that come into the country from Europe, are subject to high import taxes that must be paid by the recipient. As a result of the high import taxes, the car seller has to price the vehicle accordingly to ensure he makes enough profit. Although I visited a few car lots, I wasn't going to buy a vehicle at any of the car lots I visited on the day. The reason I visited the car lots, was to get quotes of the cost of buying a vehicle and use those quotes as estimates to take into consideration when making a decision about whether or not to set up a tour company.

During my second time in Gambia, I broke up with Ayesha. This gave me a bit more time to concentrate on doing my research on business opportunities in Gambia. I met up on a few occasions with Lady M's husband, Kebba. He fitted into my tour company idea because he used to be a tour guide and he would have been able to give local knowledge about Gambia. Another reason why I thought Kebba would be useful, is because he holds a driving licence. Therefore, I would have had him drive the tour vehicle. This would have saved me money from having to pay an additional person money to be the driver. It would have also given me an additional passenger/customer seat to utilise. And, I wouldn't have had to spend time trying to recruit a reliable driver. I felt more comfortable about going into business with Kebba rather than other locals. This was partly because of Kebba's connection with Lady M.

In my interactions with Kebba, he did strike me as a genuine person. But like with any business, there are always risks involved and you have to make an assessment of these risks. In terms of doing business with Kebba, a potential risk would have been that he may have tried to take advantage of a situation for his own financial gain. Although what I mentioned in my last sentence could be said about doing business with people in any country, it applies more in countries like Gambia because the majority of the country's population are poor and in need of financial support.

People may like or love you but if an opportunity arises that favours them, people will act on it because they're acting based on their survival and they're looking for a way out of their situation of poverty. If you're not careful enough when doing business with native Gambians, you may become the victim of their hustle. If you set up a business in Gambia, it's best for you to be in Gambia to manage the business yourself rather than manage the business from abroad. I know people who have had businesses in Gambia but lived abroad. On several occasions, business owners have had their business mismanaged by Gambians who were left in control of the business.

Gambia is a developing country. This has pros and cons for an entrepreneur (compared to doing business in Europe or USA). On the plus side, there is potential because the business sector is less saturated than in England or USA. That is good for an entrepreneur because it means there is less competitors. A big benefit of doing business in Gambia, is that it's much cheaper to rent premises in Gambia compared to Europe or USA. Business taxes are also much cheaper in Gambia. Another advantage of doing business in Gambia, is the good exchange rates you get from foreign currencies including money from Europe and USA.

Unlike Gambia, there is a huge change in traditional spending habits in Europe and USA. This is because more people are buying goods online. Therefore, the retail industry in England and USA is on a massive decline. Major high street retailers have gone out of business over the last decade in England. Whilst in the USA, there has been a lot of shopping malls that have ceased trading in recent years. Despite many shops going out of business, shop rental prices remain very high. Over the years, there has been an increase in inflation which means people have less disposable income. In England, traditional local markets are becoming nonexistent. It's a tough time to set up a retail business with a physical shopfront in England or USA. Most independent retail businesses go out of business within their first few years of trading.

In Gambia, the majority of businesses still operate in-store only with no online presence. So, it will probably be best for you to operate a business with a physical shopfront if you plan to have a retail business in Gambia. Unless, you have an online retail business where most your sales are coming from abroad. Outside the capital Banjul, most roads in Gambia don't have street names. With this being the case, an online business which delivers products could be challenging because you may not be able to find someone's address or you may spend too much time trying to get to your destination. Another problem you may face with an online business, is taking payments online. This is because most transactions in Gambia are done in cash and the majority of Gambians don't have bank cards.

The economy of Gambia is very weak. Unemployment is high and the majority of people get paid low wages. A typical monthly wage in Gambia is equivalent to around £40 per month. Hence, a lot of Gambians are struggling financially and they can't afford luxuries. If you're thinking of selling products which aren't essential, you may struggle because the *average Gambian* has either very little or no disposable income.

Many Gambians rely on remittance from relatives abroad. The majority of Gambians who are wealthy, make up a minority of the country's population. Most of the wealthy Gambians have made their fortune by working abroad or they have inherited their wealth. In Gambia, a lot of people are self-employed or work for their families or people they know. Many of the poor Gambians have business ideas but they often lack finances to implement their plans or develop their business to a higher level.

Tourism is one of the main industries that generates money for the Gambian economy. A lot of foreigners have businesses which operate during the tourist season from October to the end of April. During the off-season, they go back to the countries where they reside for the rest of the year. In Gambia, popular businesses that people often set up to cater for tourists are bars, restaurants, holiday rental accommodation, and retail shops.

Going to Gambia and having a way to make money from abroad by working online on your laptop or phone is a good idea because it's likely you will be getting paid in a stronger currency (e.g. pounds, dollars or euros). If that's the case, that's a massive benefit because the money you will be getting paid in foreign currency will be more valuable in Gambia because of the foreign exchange rates and the lower cost of living in Gambia. Nowadays, there is many opportunities to earn money from working online. This is great for people relocating to Gambia because it means you have the flexibility of where you live.

Something to take into consideration is internet access to operate your online business. In Gambia, Wi-Fi is more expensive than in England. Internet speeds are also much slower in Gambia than in England. Wi-Fi is a luxury item in Gambia. Most native Gambians can't afford to pay the upfront monthly cost for Wi-Fi. So, they top up their phones with small credit on a pay as you go basis, convert the credit into data, and use the data on their phone to go on the internet. Alternatively, they connect to the internet when they're in places that have a Wi-Fi connection.

If you are staying in Gambia for a lengthy time (especially if you have limited internet access where you're staying or you run an online business), I recommend getting a mobile Wi-Fi device because it gives you access to internet on your laptop or phone wherever you go. Purchase an unlimited data plan, so you can access the internet as much as you desire without having to worry about being capped for data. By doing that, it will also save you money from having to buy phone credit to use data on your phone.

If you're going to set up a business in Gambia, the list below are some good ideas:

- A business that sells essential products (supermarket, mini market, convenience shop, or pharmacy).

- A business catered to tourists or repats such as a hotel, restaurant, bar, or club.

- An online business that you can run by living in Gambia (preferably with money being paid in pounds, dollars or euros).

- A carwash. Cars often get dirty because of the dusty and dirt roads. Therefore, people need to wash their cars often to keep their cars in good condition (especially during rainy season). There are plenty of taxi drivers in Gambia and taxi drivers want to keep their cars in good condition for their customers (particularly tourist taxi drivers). Most carwashes in Gambia are basic. You could choose to start off with an entry level carwash, or you could have a carwash that offers a higher quality service.

- An independent builder or a construction company. There is a lot of building construction taking place and there is a need for more skilled builders to carry out the works. The influx of people from the diaspora who are moving to Gambia, is accelerating the demand for builders.

- A Laundrette. Most people in Gambia don't have washing machines. People in Gambia hand wash their clothes. Having a laundrette gives an efficient alternative for people to wash their clothes. People from the diaspora who are in Gambia or moving to Gambia, will likely find this service useful because they are more familiar with washing their clothes in a washing machine, rather than hand washing their clothes.

- A farming business. Gambia imports a lot of produce from other countries but there is an abundant of agricultural land in Gambia, which could be used more productively in regards for farming.

- You could purchase an apartment or house

and then rent out your property to visitors who are going to Gambia on holiday. Gambia is a very popular tourist destination and people need a place to stay during their time in Gambia.

- An independent land seller, estate agent, or an affiliated agent of one of the property companies that are in Gambia. With the growing influx of people from the diaspora moving to Gambia, there is a high demand of people interested in purchasing land, buying houses and renting properties in Gambia. However, you need to be very careful as a newbie selling land or property in Gambia. Make sure you are familiar with the laws, or you may be unaware that you are conducting your business affairs illegally. You also need to be very careful who you do business with because there are land scammers in Gambia.

CHAPTER 4

The second time I was in Gambia, I stayed at Palm Beach Hotel. That accommodation is only a five minutes walk away from Badala Park hotel, where I stayed the first time I was in Gambia. Therefore, I came across some of the hotel staff and locals that I met on my first stay in Gambia. On one occasion, I was walking past the craft shop where I bought my Rastafari hat during my first time in Gambia. When I was walking past the shop, I didn't think the guy who sold me the hat would recognise me. But the young man called Sailou remembered me. Sailou introduced me to his friend and colleague Modou. The hats I saw displayed on sell at their shop, had been handmade by Modou.

During my second time in Gambia, one of my aims was to get an insight into what everyday life is like for *the average Gambian*. So, I spent some time with Sailou and Modou. They took me to the village where they live. It was about a 45 minutes drive from their shop in Kotu to the village where they live. They first took me to this huge agricultural land and I met Modou's mum and sister who were farming on a small part of the land. We ate some lemons which had grown on the land and they gave me a bag full of lemons to take back with me. As we were walking through the land, I was amazed at how big it was. Sailou told me that they grow different foods on the land and that they also utilise the herbs that grow on the land. There was a part of the land where I saw lots of goats.

After we left the agricultural land, we drove to the nearby compound where Modou lives. I had some Gambian food at the compound and then he gave me a tour me of his home. Modou's bedroom and living room are of a reasonable size. I remember that the lighting in his house was very dim; that made me think that his electricity supply had low voltage. Another thing I noticed, was that there was no running water in the building. So, if he wanted to get water, he would have had to get a bucket, go outside his house to the borehole, and fill the bucket with water from the borehole. Modou's toilet and washing area was outside at the back of where he lives. There was no shelter there, I just saw an outdoor space with a hole in the ground. I remember thinking to myself that it must be very inconvenient for Modou if he needs to go toilet and it's raining (particularly in the rainy season when there is heavy rainfall). I also remember thinking it must be difficult for him to navigate to the toilet during the night because of the darkness. If Modou needs to go toilet at night, I would assume that he would have to carry a lamp or something that projects light, so that he can see where he's going.

On my way back to the hotel, I talked to Modou and Sailou about this girl who I met earlier in the day. She's called Banna. I took a liking to Banna and I knew Modou and Sailou knew her because I saw them speaking to her earlier. I asked if they could set me up with her. They said one of their friends knew her better than them and he was back at their shop (near the area she has her stall). So, they called him on the phone and he put her on the phone to speak to me. I spoke to Banna and we arranged to go out later that evening.

Earlier that day, I met Banna when I was walking in the area near the hotel. I had just left Modou and Sailou at their shop and I was heading to get something from the local mini mart. As I was walking, I turned around and I saw

Banna speaking to them briefly before she continued walking whilst carrying her lunch. I remember looking back at Banna, she stood out to me because she looked very pretty. Banna has a nice slim figure and beautiful dark black skin.

When I first saw her, I assumed she was in her 20s or early 30s. As she was walking behind me, I slowed down and I started talking to her. I needed to use a phone with a Gambian SIM card, so I could make a call to let Adama know I was back in Gambia. I used that as an excuse to speak to Banna. She agreed to let me use her phone and we went back to her stall. When I got to her stall, I found out she works as a self-employed sales agent for Africell (a phone company) selling phone credit. That was an irony because during the time I met Banna, my job was working for a phone company selling products such as phone credit (in England).

I used Banna's phone to call Adama. Then, I went to the mini mart around the corner from her stall to get what I needed whilst she went to pray. Like the majority of native Gambians, Banna is Muslim. She prays at different times in the day. When I came back from the mini mart to see Banna at her stall, we sat down and had a short conversation before I left her to get my lunch. I was glad that I was able to speak to

Banna again later that day, when I was with Modou and Sailou.

In the evening, I took Banna out to dinner at Mosiah's. We enjoyed each other's company, so we decided to meet up the next day. When I saw her the following day after she finished work, I went to her family compound where she lives. Banna's brother picked us up and took us to their family compound in Manjai. When I got to the compound, I was introduced to other members of Banna's family including her mum, her dad, her sister, and her younger nieces and nephews. Everyone was very welcoming to me. I even took several pictures with them. Banna told me that she had other siblings that lived in other places. One of her brothers lived in England.

There was a language barrier with speaking to Banna's mum because she doesn't speak English. Banna is from the Mandinka tribe. So, Banna and her mum taught me some words and phrases in Mandinka. Banna's dad was sick but he held himself in a dignified manner. I only saw Banna's dad briefly because he was in another part of the compound. I spent some time watching television with Banna and her family before Banna and I went out to dinner at a local Gambian restaurant. Banna recommended the restaurant because she had been there before.

It was a good choice because the food at the restaurant tasted nice.

The next day, Banna and I went to see Adama. In the area Lamin, Adama has a hospital. Adama is known as Adama "Dalasi" because he has a hospital where he allows people to get treatment for just 1 dalasi (less than 2 pence). I didn't get to see Adama's hospital the first time I was in Gambia because I was doing other things when Lady M and the others went to visit the hospital. However, I was able to visit the hospital during my second time in Gambia. At Adama's hospital, they use herbs and natural remedies to heal people.

Due to his hospital, Adama "Dalasi" is famous in Gambia. But I didn't know that Banna and her family knew of Adama until I brought him to their family compound with me. Neither did Banna's family know that I knew Adama. Therefore, Banna and her mum were pleasantly surprised when I brought Adama to their compound. Before we got to the hospital, Adama took us to a site near the hospital which was in the process of being built. Adama told me that he was expanding by building a new hospital. Banna and I toured the area which was under construction. I was very impressed with the development taking place and Adama's vision for his new hospital. Afterwards, Adama took us to his nearby hospital which is currently in operation.

When we got to the hospital, there were a lot of people there. Many people were outside sitting or lying down in the shade under the big tree. We spent some time at the hospital and I took some pictures with some of the patients. We spent about half an hour at the hospital before we went to Adama's house. I remember Adama's house being spacious and modern. It looked like a new build house. I liked the living room style; the furniture was nice and he had a large screen television. Adama showed me his room; he had his own en-suite bathroom.

When I spoke to Adama in his room, he told me that Banna's a good girl and he hopes that things work out between Banna and I. He also told me that he looks at me as a brother and he wants me to be happy with no problems. After Adama finished speaking with me, he had a private conversation with Banna. I noticed that one of the ladies at Adama's house gave Banna a headscarf for Banna to cover her hair before she went into Adama's room to speak with him. Banna covering her hair had something to do with the Islamic faith that her and Adama follow.

After they finished their brief conversation, Banna and I sat together in the front room and watched some television. Adama offered us some food but we didn't have any. There were some other people outside the house, so Adama was in and out of the house. Adama introduced me to the other people that were outside. One of the guys was a Gambian that had comeback from living in Sweden. After a couple of hours, Banna and I left Adama's house.

One of Adama's drivers took Banna and I to Calypso Bar and Restaurant, which is located on Cape Point beach. The restaurants seating area was under a tree hut. We had a nice view overlooking the sea. The surrounding area was very quiet; there were only a few people around. But I liked the relaxed environment. The food at Calypso Bar and Restaurant was okay but it was expensive compared to the other restaurants I had been to in Gambia. Banna's brother picked us up after we finished dinner and he dropped me back at the hotel.

On Friday that week, I took Banna to Dominos Beach Bar and Restaurant. The building leads onto a beach and there was a party being held on the beach that night. Whilst Banna and I were at Dominos, we were joined by Sailou and Modou. I also bumped into a few of the guys who worked at the hotel I stayed at during my first time in Gambia. Throughout the night at Dominos, DJ Ninja was playing reggae music. On the stage wall, there was a painting of a lion and the Rastafari colours red, gold and green.

The song that stood out to me that night was "Africa Awaits" by Mackeehan featuring Duane Stephenson. In that song, the reggae artist said: "I know a place we can be free yeah... Not here (the West) where we are bound with mental slavery yeah... Come here, I'll take you to this land (Africa)... Don't fear, everyone can come along yeah... Africa awaits, awaits, awaits her children come home... Mama Africa awaits, awaits, awaits her children come home." That song resonated with me because it's in-line with my views of the Western world and repatriation to Africa.

People of African heritage living in the diaspora must return to our ancestral homeland Africa. We must work alongside our brothers and sisters on the continent to help with the development of *the motherland*. Africa is the richest continent in the world in terms of natural resources. In contrast, Africa is the poorest continent in the world economically. That needs to change and it's going to take Africans on the continent and people of African heritage in the diaspora working together to bring about that change.

Like my first time in Gambia, the week I spent in Gambia during my second time also felt as if I was in the country double the length of the time I was there. When I got back to England, Banna and I initially kept in contact. Sadly, one of her brothers passed away and her dad's condition had got worse. At one point, Banna's dad went into hospital. Meanwhile in England, I was very busy with my job and writing my debut book *The Rise of Rastafari: Resistance, Redemption & Repatriation*. As Banna and I had a lot going on in our own lives and due to us being thousands of miles away from each other, we gradually communicated less and less until we stop messaging each other completely. We didn't fall out but I think we both realised that although we had a great time when we were together in Gambia, it would probably be best to just leave it at that.

PART 3: MY SIX MONTHS LIVING IN GAMBIA

CHAPTER 5

After two great holidays in Gambia and with my desire to be in Africa, I decided that I would go to Gambia for six months and then decide whether to go back to England or stay in Gambia after the six months. I used my savings and earnings from work to move to Gambia. I was excited and optimistic about the journey I was about to embark on. I felt very comfortable about moving to Gambia because I had already been there twice on holiday and I had made a lot of connections with people in Gambia whilst I had previously visited the country. I also had people in England who gave me contacts of people in Gambia that I could met up with.

On 2 July, 2019, I arrived in Gambia my third

time. When I got to the airport, I was picked up by one of my friends. Like me, she was born in England. After spending many years travelling back and forth between England and Gambia, she decided to permanently move to Gambia. Her parents are from the Caribbean and she was initially planning to retire in the Caribbean. But after spending time in Gambia, she fell in love with *the smiling coast of Africa*. Therefore, she chose to settle in Gambia for her retirement instead of the Caribbean. She is currently renting accommodation whilst her house is being built.

My friend's driver took us to my apartment in Bijilo. I lived there for the duration of my six months in Gambia. Once I arrived at my apartment, I was greeted by a cute young lady named Awa. As the property manager was unavailable to meet me, she gave Awa the responsibility of giving me the door key to my flat. When I arrived, Awa showed me to my apartment. We started a conversation and we also exchanged numbers with each other. Awa owns the hair salon downstairs from the apartment that I was renting.

Shortly after my friend and I arrived at my apartment, we went to three supermarkets where I did my food and household shopping. I was surprised at how expensive the products were in the supermarkets. I saw some of the brands I was familiar with seeing at shops in England. But those brands were more expensive in the Gambian supermarkets. The reason why many products are more expensive in Gambian supermarkets, is because the high import taxes Gambian businesses have to pay on importing these products from abroad.

After we got back from shopping, my friend and I went to a restaurant for dinner. We got into a shared taxi from the highway outside my flat. Along the way, the driver picked up other passengers. On main roads, you can put your hand out for a taxi and you will be picked up if there is enough space for you to get in the taxi. Alternatively, you can book a private taxi but they are a lot more expensive than a shared taxi.

Local taxis are yellow and tourist taxis are green. Sometimes green taxi drivers operate for locals as well as tourists. This often happens during off-season because there are less tourists. When green car taxi drivers operate as local drivers, their prices are cheaper than the rates they charge tourists. Private taxi prices aren't fixed; taxi drivers will often quote you a high first price. But you can usually bring the price down to a lower price if you're not happy with the initial price the driver quoted you. Taxi drivers tend to try to charge higher prices to foreigners and women. If you're out with a native Gambian, its best to get them to negotiate the price for you (particularly if they're a male).

When I was out on my own or with a woman and I needed a taxi, I spoke to the driver and negotiated the price before getting in the taxi (unless it was one of my regular taxi drivers). If the driver told me a price that I thought was too expensive, I negotiated with the driver for a cheaper price. If the driver offered me another price and I was still unhappy with the price, then I got into another taxi that accepted the price I was willing to pay. On most occasions when the taxi driver saw me about to leave him, the driver called me back and accepted the price I proposed.

When my friend and I got to the restaurant, I was immediately impressed with the modern design of the restaurant and how tidy the place was. We both ordered a burger and chips from the menu; the food tasted very good. I talked to my friend about her experience of living in Gambia. After our meal and conversation, her taxi driver dropped me back to my flat. At 11pm in the evening, I was lying down on the couch watching television. Although it was getting late at night and I had a busy day travelling, I was feeling energetic and I didn't feel like going to sleep anytime soon. So, I decided to call Awa. During our conversation on the phone, I asked her where she lives. Then, she told me to go onto the balcony outside my front door. When I went onto the balcony, I could see her flashing the light from her phone and standing on the balcony where she lived. Coincidentally, she lived around the corner from me. I invited Awa to my apartment and she came over to keep me company for a little while.

Awa told me that the building where I lived was a relative new building and that she had been running her hair salon downstairs for a few months. I liked the modern design of the building. My apartment was fully furnished, so I was able to move into my apartment without having to bother about buying a bed, furniture or a television. My rent also included security and house cleaning. The security guard was at the building at all times and once a week, the cleaner used to come to clean my flat and change the bedding. Another benefit of where I stayed, was that downstairs there was a mini mart open 24 hours a day, seven days a week. The disadvantages of my apartment were that the place didn't have an electric generator or a washing machine. There used to be power cuts and issues with the water supply sometimes. I used to have spare water bottles just in case there was no water coming from the tap.

My apartment was in a prime location, just off the popular Bertil Harding Highway in Bijilo. It takes five minutes to walk from where I was staying to Bijilo Beach. Bijilo Apartments (where I stayed) is opposite the Chamber of Commerce, and on the same road as the African Union office and the Economic Community of West African States (ECOWAS) building. Bijilo Apartments is a central location that is 10 minutes drive away from the main tourist area (Senegambia) and a five minutes drive away from the busy local area called Turntable.

The monthly cost of my apartment was 16,000 dalasi (approximately £250 per month). In Gambia, it is standard procedure to pay the full duration of your rental period before you move into a property. I had to give a small deposit of my rent to take the flat off the market. Then, I paid the remaining balance when I moved in. There was no security deposit or any other fees that I had to pay.

A fully furnished one bedroom flat like the property I had at Bijilo Apartments, is likely to cost more money in just one month's rent in a prime location in London compared to the cost of how much I paid to rent my apartment for six months in Gambia. And, there is no property in London that can match the breathtaking view of the surrounding area that I had from my Bijilo apartment. I used to wake up in the morning to the bright sun and look out the window or go onto the balcony and see beautiful palm trees. Beyond the palm trees, I could see a little bit of the sea at the top.

On my second day back in Gambia, I explored the local area. I went to visit Sailou at his shop. Before I got to the shop, I saw Banna. I didn't arrange to see Banna but I had to pass her stall on the way to get to Sailou's shop. So, I thought I might as well catch up with her and have a chat. During our conversation, she told me she had a tough time over the last few months. She had been grieving over the death of one of her brothers and her dad was still very ill. Banna knew I was coming back to Gambia but she told me her mind was focused on her family. I was sympathetic to Banna because of the death of her brother and her dad's illness.

Banna also said that she thought about us and that because I wasn't a Muslim, it would be difficult for us to have a future together because she would want me to convert to Islam and she knew that I was strongly opposed to that and it wouldn't happen. Banna's parents are both devout Muslims. Although her family liked me, she told me that her parents wouldn't accept me as her husband if I didn't convert to Islam (if we got married). As Banna is very obedient to her parents, she wouldn't marry someone without her parent's consent. Therefore, she didn't see a future in our relationship and she didn't want to waste my time. It was good to speak with Banna and clear things up. We remained friends. During my third time in Gambia, I used to visit her every once in a while, when I was in the area where she had her stall.

After catching up with Banna, I went to Sailou's shop. Sailou and I sat down and drank some green tea. Sailou told me that Modou had gone back to help his family in the village during the tourist off-season (which runs between the start of May until mid-October). Whilst I was with Sailou, I noticed that local businesses in the tourism industry such as hotels, bars and restaurants were shut. The area was very quiet; there were very few cars or pedestrians on the road.

After spending time with Sailou, I met up with Bounty. When I spoke to Bounty, he told me what he had been doing during the tourist off-season and how he was trying to manage with the odd job here and there. I took Bounty to my apartment; we watched some television and YouTube videos when we got there. I showed him the music video of the song "Gambia" by Bud Sugar. The music video was recorded in

Gambia by an English music group. Two of the artists in the group are brothers who are mixed race. When growing up, each year their mum used to take them from England to Gambia, so the boys could meet their father. I showed Bounty that video because it was recorded in Gambia, so I knew he would be familiar with some of the places in the music video. Bounty stayed with me for a little while before leaving to take care of some business. During my third time in Gambia, I met up with Bounty a few other times. I visited the compound in Manjai where he lives, we went to Serrekunda Market together, and I also met up with him on another occasion.

On my second evening at Bijilo Apartments, I met up with Awa and she introduced me to two of her friends that worked in the mini mart downstairs from my apartment. Awa, Assan, Njie and I sat outside the mini mart talking. I didn't understand a lot of what they were saying that evening because they weren't speaking in English most of the time. However, they came across friendly and humble. They were mainly speaking in Wolof (the native language of Gambia) unless they were speaking to me.

There are many different tribes in Gambia. The main tribes are Wolof, Mandinka and Fulani. The majority of Gambians are Mandinka but Wolof is the most spoken language in the country. If you look at the map of Africa, you will see that Gambia is a small country on the map that is surrounded by Senegal. The two countries were divided by the British and the French. The British colonised Gambia and the French colonised Senegal. The geographical size and population of Senegal is much bigger than Gambia. In Senegal, Wolof is the largest tribe and most spoken language. Senegalese and Gambians often travel between the two countries. So, sharing the common language of Wolof makes it easy for them to communicate with each other.

Most Gambians speak English and at least one or two native tribal languages. There are intermarriages between Gambians of different tribes. Due to the patriarchal structure of families in Gambia, the child takes on the tribe of their father. Polygamy is common in Gambia (particularly amongst the elder generations) because of the dominant Islamic culture which thrives in Gambia.

On my third day in Gambia (during my third time in the country), Kebba came to visit me with his brother Giggs. Kebba travelled three hours from his village to get to my apartment. Shortly after Kebba and Giggs arrived at my place, I took them to a local shop which had furniture and office equipment. I wanted to buy a cabinet to go in my apartment, so I took Kebba and Giggs with me because I knew that they would be able to help me negotiate a better price with the person at the shop compared to if I went on my own and tried to negotiate a deal. In Gambia, at some places of business (markets, stalls, small independent shops) they often give foreigners higher prices than the natives. If you don't speak to the person you're doing business with in one of the native languages, the person will know you come from abroad.

I remember when I was preparing to go back to England from Gambia (December 2019), I went to Serrekunda Market to buy a suitcase. Whenever I went to that market, I always took a local with me. On this occasion, I took a woman I was *seeing* (Maria) to go to the market with me. I was looking for a new suitcase because my suitcase zip had broken. I found a suitcase I wanted in one of the shops at the market. The shop owner originally quoted me 1,800 dalasi (approximately £26). Maria helped negotiate the price with the shop owner on my behalf. She spoke to the shop owner in Wolof and then Maria asked me, "How much do you want to pay for the suitcase?". I replied to Maria by saying, "900 dalasi" (approximately £13).

I thought the shop owner would decline my first offer. However, Maria spoke to the shop owner and I was pleasantly surprised that the shop owner agreed with the price I offered him. I was delighted to get the suitcase for half the initial price the shop owner quoted; not all the time the shop owner will agree to sell their product for half the price. But it's a good *rule of thumb* to begin negotiations by offering them half the first asking price they quote you. Then, barter with them by gradually increasing your offer until you agree upon a price that you're both willing to settle with. I usually went into negotiations trying to get at least 20-25% reduced from the first asking price I would be offered.

During my first and second time in Gambia, I was more generous. I didn't mind paying the full price for goods or services that I knew I could get for a cheaper price. But when I was living in Gambia for six months, my mentality was opposite. I tried to get things as cheap as possible and I was a lot more careful of how I spent my money. I was determined not to let anyone rip me off. I didn't mind paying more when I was on holiday because I was a tourist, so I was happy to pay tourist prices to support the people and the Gambian economy. But when I was living in Gambia, I was an African living in Africa (just like everyone else). For that reason, I wasn't going to pay tourist prices. On a few occasions, I made myself vocal to some people about this.

CHAPTER 6

When travelling around Gambia, you see positive images of black people in the media and on different types of advertisements. This is good because it can help to build a person's racial self-esteem when they see people that look like them represented often and in a positive way. If people don't see people of their own racial background in the spotlight, people will start to look up to the people in the spotlight who are of another racial background. As a result, people will have low racial esteem and may value themselves less.

What I liked about being in Gambia, was being in a predominately black society, seeing black people in positions of power, and seeing black owned businesses everywhere I went. As a black man, I felt like I was at home and in a normal environment with no racial bias. It was like the total opposite of being in England, where I feel like an outsider because the majority of the population is white and the society is racist towards non-whites, especially to blacks.

In England, black people are a very small percentage of the population. In most English cities or towns, you will only see a few if any black owned businesses on the main high streets (especially outside the major cities). There isn't big corporations or industry leading businesses that are black owned. Black people are put at the bottom of the society and are held back from progressing into positions of power because of institutional racism.

Black people in England don't have enough power to bring about big changes that affect the day-to-day reality of most black people living in the country in a way which empowers black people to thrive in the society. The government, educational institutions, police, military, and multi-billion pound companies are controlled by another race of people that are working against the collective interests of black people. There is only a small number of black people in high positions of power and these people are either *house negroes*, sell-outs, or they have white partners.

In Gambia, you are valued by your character and how you conduct yourself. You are treated accordingly for who you are as a person, not because of the colour of your skin. In Gambia, I never felt out of place because everywhere I went people welcomed me and accepted me for who I am. Therefore, I felt more appreciated in Gambian society compared to English society. I blended in with Gambians and the country's environment straight away, almost as if I was born and raised in Gambia.

The Western world has much to learn from Gambia in terms of morals, values, and how human beings should treat one another. Gambia and African societies in general are based on the principle of Ubuntu, which is a word from the Bantu language. Ubuntu means "I am because we are". Gambian society is more collective rather than individualistic. It's a big contrast to Western societies that are *dog-eat-dog capitalist societies,* where people look out for number one (themselves) at all costs.

Gambians are kind, helpful, caring, and protective. The third time I arrived in Gambia was during the rainy season. One evening, it rained very heavily. I was coming back home from a nightclub. When the car got near my apartment, the taxi driver and I saw that the path I needed to get to my flat was waterlogged.

The taxi driver had to park his taxi across the road from my apartment because of the high volume of water that was blocking the pathway to my flat.

As I still needed to go past the rainfall to get home, the driver kindly offered to walk through the water and carry me on his back so I could get to my flat. I was pleasantly surprised by this kind gesture, especially because the size difference between us. I'm a big man who is six foot three inches tall and also broad. The taxi driver was average height and he was slim. I was grateful that the taxi driver offered to carry me through the rainfall. However, I decided to go across the water by myself. I got soaked up to my knees but I thought this was the better option because I believe my weight would have been too much for the taxi driver to carry me, so we would have fallen in the water.

I recall another time when it had been raining and the water puddles made it difficult to cross the road. I was being picked up by one of my friends. Her taxi driver parked across the road, got out the car, crossed the road, took my bags across the road with him, and then guided me through crossing the road. The kind of service you get from taxi drivers in Gambia, is far superior to the service you get from taxi drivers in England.

My mental health was much better in Gambia compared to how it was before I moved there from England. Both my anxiety and obsessive-compulsive disorder (OCD) cured naturally whilst I was in Gambia. I also felt in a much better mood in Gambia compared to how I felt in England. I believe this was down to me being in a less stressful environment and being in a place I felt relaxed, peaceful, and a valued person in the society. I had a very active lifestyle in Gambia, this helped my overall well-being. I also lost weight during my six months in Gambia. The pace of life in Gambia is much slower compared to England; things are more laid-back in Gambia. Walking through the streets in Gambia, I felt so much freedom. In England, I always feel restrained everywhere I go.

I hate the way how in England everything has to be done so formal and *long-winded*; things are often overcomplicated through procedures, systems, and protocols. In Gambia, things are more straightforward and less complicated compared to how things are done in England. For example, on one occasion I needed to get a tin number (equivalent to a UK tax number) to set up a bank account in Gambia. It was a simple and quick procedure to get my tin number: (1) I went to the relevant office that deals with issuing tin numbers, (2) I showed them my identification, (3) I filled out a short form. It took 10-15 minutes from the time I arrived at the office, to the time I got my tin number.

It was also a simple procedure extending my stay in Gambia: (1) I went into the immigration office, (2) I paid the fee to extend my stay, (3) I got my passport stamped. As a British passport holder, I didn't need a visa to enter Gambia. A British passport holder is allowed to stay in Gambia for 30 days from the date they enter the country. If they wish to extend their stay after that period, they must extend their stay by going to one of the immigration offices in Gambia. The first time I needed to extend my stay, I went to the immigration office in Senegambia. They weren't managing passport extensions from that office. So, the immigration officer kindly took me to the immigration office in Serrekunda to get my passport stamped.

When I got to Serrekunda, I met the head immigration officer. He asked me how long I planned to be in the country. I replied to him by saying, "6 months". He told me that I could extend my stay in the country for six months. I paid to extend my stay for three months because that was the amount of money in cash that I had on me. At the end of the three months, I went back to extend my stay again.

On both occasions when I went to extend my stay at the immigration offices, the officers were friendly and they treated me well. I wasn't interrogated and I didn't have to fill out any forms. During the second time I went to extend my passport in Serrekunda, I was even offered to eat lunch with the officers at the station. In Gambia, part of the community culture is based on sharing. People share food amongst their relatives, their work colleagues, their friends, people in the community, and with strangers they don't know.

In the Western world, people are *slaves to the system* (this applies to all ethnicities). I do not believe I was put on earth to work for an employer eight hours a day, five days a week, and spend two hours of my time on work travel every day. Neither do I believe I was put on earth to go to work for a company every day and have to listen to someone tell me what to do, when I can eat, and when I can go home. In the West, people's lives are dictated around work. People have little social time to spend with their family or friends because of their busy work schedule. People get home from work feeling tired. Then, they eat, they have a couple hours of spare time, and then they go to sleep before they get up to do the same routine day in, day out. People work so hard doing their jobs (many people also have to spend hours commuting), so that on their day/s off they just want to rest.

In England, it's common for workplaces to be very demanding and stressful environments. I have spent seven years working in the sales industry for different companies. I was a best-seller at all the sales companies I worked for and I was the best retail sales agent in the country for one of those companies. But even though I was the best at my job in the country, I still faced racial discrimination.

CHAPTER 7

During my third time in Gambia, I went into two schools and delivered three lectures about my debut book *The Rise of Rastafari: Resistance, Redemption & Repatriation*. My Gambian friend Abdoulie was a teacher at the time. So, I spoke to him about going to do lectures in schools and he arranged that for me in a matter of days. Abdoulie was the deputy headteacher at a school for young adults. I delivered a lecture there and I also delivered two lectures to two classrooms full of younger students at another school that Abdoulie previously taught at.

In England, it's not as straightforward as it is in Gambia when arranging a lecture in a school or an educational institution. This is because you have to follow a long procedure in England. To begin with, you will need to draft a proposal.

Then, you will need to get formal permission from the subject teacher. Following this, the subject teacher will need to get permission from the head of department, and that person may need to get permission from the deputy or head teacher. The topic you plan to speak about must fit into the school curriculum and you may be restricted to what you can say and how you wish to deliver your lecture.

You could be waiting several weeks or months to hear back from the school (that's if they choose to respond). If your proposal has been approved, it's likely you're going to have to wait at least a few weeks before you can go into the school and deliver the lecture. Before you are allowed to go into school to talk to students, you will need to undergo a DBS check and your record must be clean. Unlike Gambia, England has a lot of pedophiles, child abusers and criminals. Therefore, English schools and other institutions check people's backgrounds before they are given access to students or vulnerable people.

Travelling around in Gambia reminded me of Jamaica. There are many similarities between Gambia and Jamaica such as how the countries look, the lovely sunny weather, the beautiful palm trees, and the magnificent beaches. Gambia's population and geographical size is also similar to Jamaica. And, Gambians love Jamaican culture. Reggae is the most popular music in Gambia. I was hearing reggae music played in the clubs, bars, restaurants, taxis, hotels, and streets. When I went clubbing in Gambia, most of the clubs were playing reggae and dancehall throughout the night. One could argue that they love reggae in Gambia even more than how much Jamaicans love reggae in Jamaica. One evening, I went to a pool party and they even had a dancehall competition to see who's *King/Queen of the dancehall*.

In Gambia, there are many young men who are reggae and dancehall DJs and music artists. There are also a lot of young Gambian men who style their hair in dreadlocks to emulate the hairstyle that is common amongst Rastafarians from Jamaica. Over the years, many famous reggae artists from Jamaica have travelled to perform in Gambia. These popular reggae stars include Chronixx, Fantan Mojah, Anthony B, Christopher Martin, and Asha Heights. I met Asha Heights when I was on my way back home from my second trip to Gambia (February 2019). Asha Heights gave me a copy of his latest music CD and I interviewed him about his experience of *the smiling coast of Africa*.

In some of the local marketplaces and shops, it's common to see clothes, hats, necklaces, and accessories in the Rastafari colours of red, gold and green. There are many young Gambians who like aspects of Rastafari culture such as dreadlocks, reggae and ganja. But Gambians have very little knowledge about what Rastafari is. The majority of Gambians think Rastafari is a hairstyle and anyone who has dreadlocks is a Rastafarian (regardless of their beliefs). When I was in Gambia, I heard several people refer to their hair or someone else's hair as "Rasta" because the hair was styled in dreadlocks.

Over 90% of the population in Gambia are Muslims. On one hand, it is good Rastafari is in Gambia at least in some capacity (albeit not it's true form) because Rastafari offers them an alternative culture to Islam. But on the other hand, it's like *a slap in the face* to Rastafari (although not intended) because people are misrepresenting Rastafari as a fashion instead of having a genuine understanding of Rastafari as a black power movement. As a result, the message of Rastafari is being tarnished.

I know Gambians who have locks, love reggae music and smoke ganja. They are Muslim and they will tell you that they are Muslim. Some of them even claim that they are Muslim and Rastafarian. But it's impossible to be a Rasta and also be a Muslim because Rastafari philosophy, principles and values are completely different to

Islam. The misrepresentation of Rastafari by young Gambians is down to ignorance rather than deliberation. Whilst I was in Gambia, I made it one of my duties to educate the native Gambians about Rastafari.

My objective was to make Gambians view Rastafari more seriously and in a positive light by getting them to understand the relevance of Rastafari to black liberation. Along with being a devout Rastafarian, I am also an author of a book about Rastafari. And, I am a Rastafari exponent, scholar, and historian. In addition to teaching Rastafari in the Gambian schools, I shared my knowledge about Rastafari with my friends and others in the local communities. I also gave out some copies of my book *The Rise of Rastafari*.

It was very emotional when I delivered my lectures in schools about Rastafari. Educating my fellow African brothers and sisters on the continent about Rastafari (including black history) were very special moments for me. I felt a sense of satisfaction within myself because of my works in passing on my knowledge of Rastafari and black history to those students. It was a joy to bring awareness of the true form of Rastafari to those students and to dispel the common misconceptions and negative things that they thought about Rastafari.

Before I went into those schools, I asked the students what they thought of Rastafari. The students had a very low opinion of Rastafari. Some of the things the students said were, "People who take drugs" and "People who don't matter (worthless people)". My friend Abdoulie told me that initially he was a bit unsure about whether to bring me into the school to talk about Rastafari because what he used to think of Rastafari was bad. But after I did my lectures and he read my book, his perspective about Rastafari changed and he could identify with Rastafari.

I got 100 copies of my book *The Rise of Rastafari* printed in Gambia. My books were printed by a printing company called Unique Graphics. They gave me a good price and I was happy with the quality of the books they printed for me. It took them about a week to get my books printed, which was a reasonable amount of time. Before I left Gambia, I donated 40 copies of my book to some of the school students.

Timbuktoo is the most popular and biggest bookshop in Gambia. I was pleasantly surprised when I visited Timbuktoo for the first time and saw the wide variety of books they had. I was particularly impressed with their section of books on black history, Pan-Africanism, African leaders, and contemporary topics relevant to people of African heritage. I saw books I have read such as *The Autobiography of Haile Selassie I, A Historical Report: The Rastafari Movement in England,* and *The Philosophy and Opinions of Marcus Garvey*. I also saw a book written by Omowale Rupert, an author I know who lives in England. His book is called *Pan-Afrikanism: The Battlefront: Afrikan Freedom Means Defeating Neo-Colonialism*.

At Timbuktoo, I bought a book about the pioneer of the Rastafari Movement, Leonard Howell. The book is called *The First Rasta: Leonard Howell and the Rise of Rastafarianism*. I managed to get copies of my book *The Rise of Rastafari* stocked at Timbuktoo. I also got copies of my book stocked at Rasville Fashion, near Turntable. Rasville Fashion is a shop that sells a variety of Rastafari themed products. The shop owner of Rasville Fashion is Joe Texx. He is also a reggae artist who has been travelling to Gambia for years. Joe Texx is of Caribbean heritage but he was living in England before he decided to settle in *the smiling coast of Africa*.

During my time in Gambia, I came across some Rastafarians (like Joe Texx) who have a lot of knowledge about Rastafari. Those people were other Rastafarians of Caribbean heritage, who were living in England before they moved to Gambia. Although Rastafari is about Pan-Africanism, Rastafari emerged as a result of the experience of Caribbean people in the diaspora. So, it's understandable why people of Caribbean heritage that I met in Gambia had a lot more knowledge about Rastafari compared to the Gambian people I met.

CHAPTER 8

During my first couple weeks of my third time in Gambia, Awa and I became close and we got into a relationship. One day, she took me to one of her friend's weddings. When we got to the venue where the wedding ceremony was taking place, I noticed that people were dressed in traditional African clothes. I was wearing a kente shirt that was designed by Jtaphrique African clothing shop. I bought that shirt in England before I moved to Gambia. At the wedding, the couple getting married were both Christians. Therefore, the wedding took place in a church.

Christianity is the second most popular religion in Gambia after Islam. Christians make up a small percentage of the population, which is under 10%. I was disappointed when I saw the paintings of white Jesus Christ on the wall at the church. I found it strange being in a black country where everyone who attends that church is black, yet the church has a white man on the wall depicted to be black people's saviour. It goes to show how Gambians are still influenced from colonialism. Almost the whole Gambian population are Muslims or Christians. It is very rare to find a Gambian that was born and raised in Gambia and that person is Atheist, Agnostic, or a traditional African spiritualist.

After the church service, Awa and I went to the outdoor venue where they held the wedding reception. The rest of the afternoon and evening was filled with entertainment such as African dancing, music, and speeches. During the day, guests went to the front to give gifts to the new married couple. There were hundreds of people at the wedding reception. Traditional Gambian foods were served throughout the day. I liked the benachin, which is Gambia's national dish. At the wedding, everyone was given their own plate to eat from. That was unlike the usual Gambian eating culture, where everyone eats together from a large bowl of food.

I liked the Gambian food that I ate at the wedding but I didn't like most Gambian foods that I ate during my time in *the smiling coast of*

Africa. Therefore, I tended to stick to food that I was more used to. This was food such as pizza, fried chicken, cereal, English bread, hot dogs, tinned fruit cocktail, snapper fish, chips, brown stew chicken, jerk chicken, curry goat, and rice and peas. My favourite restaurants in Gambia were CK in Bijilo, Spanglers near Turntable, and Mosiah's in Kotu.

Spanglers is a Jamaican restaurant like Mosiah's (now Mo2). CK is a restaurant and bakery, which has a mixture of Gambian foods and different types of fast food that I was familiar with. Although I didn't like most Gambian foods I tasted, there is a drink called Youki (fruit cocktail) that is manufactured in Gambia. I love that drink and wish they sold Youki in more countries outside Gambia.

After Awa and I got back from the wedding, I bumped into one of the guys who works at the car park outside the building where I lived. The guy introduced me to his friend and work boss Aladin (owner of the car business). They sell cars and repair cars at the car park. I spoke to them briefly on that occasion but over time I got to know them well. They are both very humble and easy-going. Aladin was born in Gambia but he'd spent most of his life in Europe. He lived in Germany, Scotland, England, Switzerland, and Austria.

Something I learned by living in Gambia and talking to the native people there, is that many of the native Gambians either have relatives living abroad or they themselves had been living abroad at some point. I watched a programme which stated that Gambia had the highest percentage of citizens who were living abroad compared to any other African country. One day at the car park, Aladin and I were sitting down. Aladin got out his photo collection and he shared some of his fond memories with me by going through his photographs. I saw pictures of him and his friends; the photos were from different locations in Europe during the periods he spent living there.

As the days and weeks went on, I got to know the other seven guys who I use to see at the car park regularly. Most of the time, they weren't altogether. I would normally see a few of them in the car park at different times. Some of them work at the car park, the others would visit the car park occasionally to chill out with the other guys who work there. I used to spend time downstairs from my flat with the guys from the car park and the guys from the mini mart. I bonded very well with them and we became close, like brothers. We used to sit down, relax, drink green tea, and discuss different things. Sometimes we would watch videos on YouTube or listen to reggae music. There were always people around to keep me company and we were all young adults between 20-40.

Awa was very busy at her salon working from early morning till late at night everyday apart from Monday (her day off). I wanted to spend more quality time with her but she didn't have much spare time away from working at her hair salon. As I didn't want to be unfaithful to Awa, I thought it would be best for us to split up. Awa and I remained good friends after we broke up. I even thought about getting back with her a couple of times because we got on very well. Awa is a very nice lady.

A couple weeks after Awa and I broke up, I started dating a pretty young Nigerian woman. I met her when I was getting food at a restaurant. When I first arrived at the restaurant, the lady was already sitting down and I had just come in. As I sat down, she caught my eye so I went over and introduced myself to her. We had a good conversation and after we finished eating our food, we went to another venue to play pool and chill out. For purposes of this book, I am going to keep that lady's name anonymous and I will refer to her as Monique.

The relationship between Monique and I started off very well but it deteriorated fast. Jealously was one of the issues between

Monique and I. She used to constantly accuse me of having another girlfriend and cheating on her. She also used to constantly accuse me of looking at other girls anytime we were out together. Although Monique is very pretty, she came across as insecure when we were dating. I also felt that she tried to test me to see how much she could control me. I stood my ground and didn't tolerate her nonsense. Therefore, we drifted apart. A couple weeks after we broke up, she changed her tune. Monique called me on the phone saying that she missed me and she apologised to me for the things that I told her that I didn't like during the time we were together. Although I left that conversation on good terms with Monique, I didn't want to get back with her because I had moved on.

A couple of months after Monique and I had broken up, I started *seeing* one of her friends. I didn't see it as an issue because Monique and I had broken up and it wasn't like Monique and I had a long-term relationship and/or we had a child together. As far as I was concerned, the relationship between Monique and I was *done and dusted*. Her friend knew exactly what the situation was with Monique and I because I spoke to Monique's friend about it. I didn't have much sympathy for Monique about the situation between her friend and I because if

Monique treated me better, I wouldn't have stopped dating her in the first place.

Monique's friend was a gorgeous young woman from Sierra Leone. She looked like a supermodel. Although I was attracted to both Monique and her friend, I would never have started *seeing* Monique's friend if Monique and I were still dating. Unfortunately, Monique's friend had a dull personality. She wasn't rude or disrespectful but she seemed shallow and she didn't have much of a character. So, I stopped *seeing* her and moved on.

One out of the many things I liked about being in Gambia, is that I got to know several *continental Africans* who had moved from other parts of West Africa to live in Gambia. I met Africans from Nigeria, Sierra Leone, Senegal, and Guinea. Gambia is part of ECOWAS; an organisation made up of West African countries which allows free movement of West African citizens to go into other countries in West Africa that are also part of ECOWAS. During my time in Gambia, I also came across a couple of people from as far as Ethiopia (East Africa). One of the Ethiopians I met, is related to Emperor Haile Selassie I.

In Gambia, like other parts of Africa, the men and the women maintain traditional roles in relationships. The man *wears the trousers* in the relationship and the woman caters for her man. The man is the head of house, leader, provider, and protector of his woman and family. The woman's role is to support and encourage her man. One evening, I was with a young lady at my flat. She wanted something to eat, so I went to the kitchen sink to wash up a bowl and spoon for her to use to eat some food. She stopped me from washing up and she insisted that she would do the washing up. She said, "Let me do it. In my culture, men don't do these things."

Like most housing in Gambia, my apartment didn't have a washing machine. Neither was there a washing machine in the building that I could use to do my laundry. Gambians normally handwash their clothes themselves or they have someone who washes their clothes for them. When I was dating Awa, she used to wash my clothes and iron them for me. I didn't make her do it; she used to offer to do it for me. I thought that was very kind of her and I appreciated it.

After a few times of Awa doing my laundry, I didn't want to burden her with having to wash my clothes because I knew Awa had a lot of stuff to do with running her hair salon and looking after her nieces whilst her sister was away in England. So, I started to do my own laundry. I used to go on the balcony at my apartment and handwash my clothes using a bucket filled with water and soap. After the clothes were washed, I hanged the clothes up to dry in the hot weather. One day, Awa was downstairs and she saw me washing my clothes on the balcony. She told me to tell her the next time that I would be doing my laundry, so she could help me do it.

I remember one time I was at Awa's house and she cooked some food for us to eat. After we ate the meal, she asked me if I wanted some ice cream. I replied, "Yes". I assumed she had ice cream in her house but she didn't. Without me knowing, Awa went to the shop and got me some ice cream. I thought it was nice that she done that. However, I would have told her not to bother getting the ice cream if I knew she had to go out the house to get the ice cream (especially as it was late at night).

Something I observed from being in Gambia, is how strong relationships are between males and females. This is whether it's the relationship between husband and wife, boyfriend and girlfriend, father and daughter, or brother and sister. There is a lot of love and respect between males and females in Gambian society. This is primarily down to the patriarchal structure that exists in Gambian families and also in Gambian society. It was so refreshing to see black males and females getting on so well. Especially as someone who had been living in England, which is a country where the black family is *breaking down*. Whilst I was in Gambia, I didn't hear women badmouthing men. Neither did I hear men badmouthing women.

In most Gambian households, both the father and mother raise the child. However, the father is acknowledged as the dominant parent and spouse. There is recognition that males and females have different roles and that males are leaders of their women. That's not to say women are weak or that women aren't valued because females are well respected in Gambia.

Gambian children have excellent behaviour, whether that be at school or outside school. I remember going into schools and seeing how well-mannered and mature the young students were. One day, I was outside with my friend and there was a child playing around. The child was the son of a black person from the diaspora who had moved to Gambia. When my Gambian friend saw the way how that child was playing around, he told me that if that child was born and raised in Africa with African parents, that child would not be playing around like how he was because that child would have discipline.

Most children and young students that I came across in Gambia seemed intelligent. One day, I went to see a debate at the University of The Gambia. It was a debate which had two teams consisting of two people on each side. I was really impressed by the level of intelligence displayed and the way how both teams presented their arguments. I met some really bright young males in Gambia. Some of those people don't hold any degrees or high-level qualifications, but they are smart.

Global affairs, history, and geography are three area's that I found the *average* Gambian didn't have much knowledge on. They know very little about world history or things currently happening in other countries over the world (apart from Gambians who have been abroad). Even in relation to current affairs in most other parts of Africa, the majority of Gambians don't know what's going on in those countries. Also, most Gambians only know a few of the names of the other African countries outside of West Africa.

CHAPTER 9

17 August is the birthday of Marcus Garvey. Rastafarians and Garveyites celebrate that date every year in honour of Marcus Garvey. I was invited by an elder Rastafarian of Jamaican heritage to deliver a talk about the importance of Marcus Garvey to the Rastafari Movement. The lady who invited me to speak had been living in England before moving to Gambia. I was introduced to this lady by my friend Dr. Aboo Rahtata from Galaxy Radio station.

I delivered my talk at Mymoonia Garden, which is a place that sells Caribbean food and they also offer other holistic health treatments. I noticed the sign outside Mymoonia Garden had the Sankofa symbol of a bird looking backwards taking an egg. Sankofa is an Adinkra symbol from the Akan tribe in Ghana. Sankofa translated in English means, "to go back and get it." It's for us to acknowledge that we must look back at the past and learn from our own (or ancestors) past, so we can be better equipped for the future by understanding how things from the past have relevance today. We must also use things we have learned from the past when necessary. One of Marcus Garvey's famous quotes is, "A man without knowledge of his past history, origin and culture is like a tree without roots."

There are beautiful paintings on the wall at Mymoonia Garden. One of the paintings I saw that stood out to me, was a painting of the *Black Star Line* ship with black people going back to Africa. I also saw a painting on the wall of the map of Africa; the painting was coloured in the Rastafari colours of red, gold and green. During the afternoon I spent at Mymoonia Garden, I met other people who had moved from the diaspora to live in Gambia. I also met a bright young Gambian called Spider. We had an interesting discussion about Haile Selassie I and Pan-Africanism. During the conversation we had, Spider came across as intelligent. He told me that he teaches young children and he occasionally organises events catered towards older teenagers and young adults.

The following day, I went back to Mymoonia

Garden to attend another event. Like the previous day, there was also many English born *African returnees* of Caribbean descent who had moved from England to Gambia. These *African returnees* created a group working together with native Gambians. Whilst at this event, I met Abdoulie for the first-time (the teacher in chapter 7). Abdoulie was one of the main people involved in the meeting that took place. Spider was also at the meeting. During the meeting, the group had a discussion about organising a health awareness event. I got on well with Abdoulie and Spider because the three of us are Pan-Africanists and educators. We have the same vision, which is to empower people of African heritage through education focused on black consciousness and matters relevant to people of African heritage.

The following week, Spider picked me up from my apartment and took me to his village in Jambanjelly. It took us about 30 minutes by car to get to our destination. On our way there, most of the journey was a straight drive on one of the highways. Whilst Spider was driving, I was looking out the window and the scenery was beautiful. Also, I noticed that the highway roads were very well paved. They had built some new roads to a high standard on the highway leading into Jambanjelly. When we got to the village, I saw that the roads in Jambanjelly were also new.

Throughout Gambia, a lot more of the roads should be improved to a better standard like the highway to Jambanjelly and the new roads in Jambanjelly. Road improvements would benefit vehicle drivers and pedestrians, particularly during the rainy season when the rain floods the roads and blocks the paths for vehicle drivers and pedestrians. During the rainy season (when it rains), it's common for vehicles to get stuck in the high volume of water and for vehicles to get damaged and/or dirty. Also, it's inconvenient for pedestrians because they may be stuck in a location until the water goes down enough for them to be able to walk. Sometimes the flooding is severe and it causes destruction to the villages.

In Jambanjelly, Spider took me to see his house and the land he owns. Spider has a large amount of land which he inherited. He grows herbs and fruits on his land. Spider gave me a bag of moringa seeds to take home with me. He also showed me the land where he's planning to develop a community centre to host events and educate the children at his school.

Spider gave me a tour around his village. He showed me the local market where people buy their food. Then, we went to watch some of the local boys playing a football match. After that, we briefly stopped by a naming ceremony. When walking around Jambanjelly with Spider, I felt comfortable and no one was looking at me as if I was a foreigner. Whilst we travelled through the village, I remember thinking that if the transatlantic slave trade never happened, this is what my life could have been like in Gambia or in another part of Africa.

The next week, Spider took me to a naming ceremony of one of his family members. This was so I could experience more of the Gambian culture. During a naming ceremony, the couple announce the name of the new-born baby. In Gambia, naming your new-born baby is a big occasion where the community comes together to celebrate it. People dress in traditional African clothes and food is provided throughout the day. People get the chance to give their blessings to the couple who have had their new-born baby. And, it's common for people to give money or a gift to the parents of the new-born baby.

I also went to the naming ceremony of Abdoulie's sister's new-born baby. The naming ceremony took place at Abdoulie's parent's house. I remember seeing a lot of people in the house when we walked in. The house was big and it looked really nice. In one of the rooms in the house, there was the maternal family of the new-born baby on one side of the room and the paternal family of the new-born baby on the other side of the room. First, the family of the baby's father were giving appreciation and respect to the family of the baby's mother. This was followed by the baby's mother's family reciprocating the gesture of respect to the family of the baby's father. In Gambia, marriages are more than just a marriage between individuals. When people marry, they marry into a family and become part of the family they marry into (not just by legality).

I enjoyed the experience of going to both of the naming ceremonies that I was invited to by Abdoulie and Spider. But I was disappointed that the new-born babies were both given Islamic names and not African names. However, I wasn't surprised about that because it's common for most people in Gambia to have Islamic names such as Abdoulie, Adama, Aji, Assan, Awa, Ebrima, Fatima, Fatou, Lamin, Modou, Mohammed, Momodou, Ousman, and Suleiman. It was refreshing being with Spider who is an atheist because almost everyone in Gambia is Muslim or Christian.

Islam has a stronghold on the majority of people's minds in Gambia. It's common for Gambians to pray three times a day. Men go to the mosque on Friday afternoons and many shops close at 1pm until 2.30pm or 3pm because of Friday prayers. Former Gambian President Yahya Jammeh declared Gambia an Islamic Republic in 2015. He legally changed Gambia's name to *Islamic Republic of The Gambia*. When the next president Adama Barrow came into office, he denounced Gambia as an Islamic Republic. In 2017, Barrow changed back Gambia's official name to *Republic of The Gambi*a.

In Gambia, a lot of people live in compounds with extended families. Society is family and community orientated. There is an African saying, "It takes a village to raise a child." In Gambia, that saying is evident because a child is born into a community and the child is treated as if it belongs to everyone in that community. Children are grown up to have respect for elders within the society. People treat their friend's mother or father as a mother or father figure to them (whenever they're in the presence of their friend's mother or father). Although their friend's mother or father is not their actual parent, the elder is treated with the same respect and dignity that the younger person would show to their own parent.

Gambia is a relatively safe place to live. I felt comfortable going out at night or day anywhere

I went in Gambia. The majority of people in Gambia were very nice to me and I didn't have any problems with crime or my security whilst I was there. I have lived in London before and in comparison, Gambia is a lot safer than living in most parts of London. I think Gambia is also a safe place for women to travel around on their own. But just like everywhere else in the word, crime does happen and there are things you can do to make yourself less vulnerable.

Burglaries are one of the most common crimes in Gambia. It is a good idea to live in a home that is fenced off and has a security gate (many houses or compounds in Gambia are like that). Another way to protect your home, is to get a security guard. In Gambia, security guards cost very little money. You can get a security guard for £40 per month. Another option is to have a security front door gate. You could also have security bars on the windows.

Gambia is a very peaceful country and most of its citizens are good people. But you can make yourself a target if you don't have your wits about you (particularly if you're a foreigner). Don't have your phone visible in a way that it may attract a robber, like leaving your phone out on display in your back pocket or walking around in the market with your phone exposed to other people nearby you. When you get into shared taxis with people you don't know, be cautious of where you put your possessions. Don't put your possessions in a pocket where they could easily fall out and don't put your possessions in a pocket where something could be easily taken from your pocket without you knowing.

Gambia is not a place to go around boasting about what you have or flaunting like you're *the best thing since sliced bread*. The first reason why you should not do this, is because it will make you a target. The second reason, is because it's inconsiderate to constantly boast or flaunt what you've got when there are many locals who are poor and don't have what you have. By constantly boasting about what you've got or flaunting it, you will appear to others as an arrogant snob. Gambians are very humble people. Even the Gambians who are rich and live in their mansions, are as humble and respectful as *the average Gambian* who is trying *to make ends meet*.

When I was in Gambia, I was able to see the gap between the rich and the poor because I knew people who were rich and others who were poor. If you have *money* in Gambia, you can *live like a king*. Some Gambians I know are so wealthy that their house is like a palace designed for royalty. Inside their house, the furniture and the decoration are of the highest quality. I had never in my life gone into homes so big and luxurious like some of the homes I went into in Gambia.

Rich Gambians drive expensive luxury cars. One day, I was outside someone's house and I saw five Range Rovers parked outside the house. Those cars were lined up one behind each other. On another day, I was in Kotu with my friend. We were outside chilling and I remember watching the cars driving past on the street. We were on the same street for about an hour. The road wasn't busy but there was a trickle of cars driving past every so often. During that time, almost every car driving past on that road was a Range Rover or another expensive luxury car. My friend and I left Kotu to go to one of the bars in Senegambia. Like how it was at the road we were on in Kotu, there were also lots of Range Rovers and expensive luxury cars driving past on this road too.

In contrast to rich Gambians, the majority of the population are poor Gambians. When I was in Gambia, I went to some people's homes and there was no running water. All they had was their clothes, a mattress on the floor to sleep on, and a few basic things. Most people in Gambia make less money working a whole month compared to how much most people in England make working just a few hours. Life in Gambia can be very hard for poor people. If you're a poor Gambian, it's an *uphill battle* to change your circumstance.

Despite there being some poverty in Gambia, I didn't feel like I was in a *third world* country or a poor country when I was in Gambia. One of the reasons why that was the case, was because I didn't see people in the streets starving. Neither did I see homeless people on the streets or even disabled people with walking sticks. People in general, looked healthy. Another reason why I didn't see Gambia as a poor country, is because the Gambians I met conducted themselves with such dignity. My final reason why I didn't see Gambia as a poor country, is because the country looks beautiful. Although the majority of Gambians are poor financially, there is a richness within Gambian people and their society, which is beyond the value of money or materialistic things.

CHAPTER 10

There is a growing number of black people from England who have either moved to Gambia to live or have businesses in Gambia. I thought it would be a good idea to make a documentary to highlight the journey of those individuals, so more people in the diaspora would be able to get an insight into life in Gambia. I had a list of people who I wanted to interview for my documentary. But I wanted to get more people to interview, so I asked people I knew if they knew anyone who they thought would be suitable to speak about their experience of Gambia in my documentary.

When planning my documentary, I had a conversation on the phone with Angela "Angie" Rose from AGA Global Ambassadors. Angie runs a charity and a tour company in Gambia. I also spoke to Dr. Aboo Rahtata from Galaxy Radio. Dr. Aboo has been to Gambia several times and he has many contacts in the country. I told Angie and Dr. Aboo about my plan of doing a documentary. They gave me some suggestions of people to contact for my documentary. One person they both mentioned was Juliet Ryan. Before coming to Gambia, Juliet and I hadn't met in-person but we were both activists within black communities in England. Therefore, we already had a lot of mutual friends. I even already knew Juliet's uncle, Ras Earl. Juliet's uncle and his wife used to go to events that were put on by Luton Black Men Community Group, an organisation that I was previously a member of. But I didn't know that Ras Earl was Juliet's uncle until I came to Gambia and found that out by speaking with Juliet.

Two weeks after I spoke to Dr. Aboo and Angie, I saw a video of Juliet being interviewed by a YouTube vlogger named Wode Maya. At that point, I still hadn't met Juliet in-person. I was familiar with Wode Maya on YouTube since I saw a video of him showing different parts of Nigeria, which was during August that year. I subscribed to Wode Maya's YouTube channel and I watched some of the other videos of him travelling around different places in Africa.

One day, I remember watching a video of

Wode Maya and I realised that he was in Gambia. Wode Maya even did a YouTube vlog about a hotel called Coco Ocean, which is near to where I was living in Bijilo. A couple days later, I saw that Juliet was on his YouTube channel speaking about why she moved from England to Gambia. Racism was the main reason she gave for her decision to relocate. Juliet said, "England is a dump". That video went viral with over a million views on the internet. Wode Maya did another video with Juliet. In that video, Juliet did a tour around her house.

Before Wode Maya left Gambia, he set up Juliet with her own YouTube channel, so that Juliet could do her own vlogging about Gambia. That was the founding of Blaxit YouTube channel. Juliet got the idea to name the YouTube channel Blaxit because of the term Brexit. The withdrawal of the United Kingdom from the European Union is called Brexit, which is the short form of saying British Exit. Blaxit is about the withdrawal of black people from the diaspora and those people moving to Africa. With the term Blaxit, the letters r and e from Brexit have been replaced with the letters l and a. Therefore, *Bla* is to represent black people and *xit* represents exit.

In the first week Blaxit was formed, I was contacted by Juliet on Facebook. We had a phone conversation in the evening and she invited me to do an interview for the Blaxit YouTube channel. We also spoke about her doing an interview for my documentary, which she agreed to do. The following day from our phone conversation, I went to Juliet's house to do my interview for Blaxit. Juliet's house looked very nice and it was a big house with several bedrooms. I was introduced to her family including her husband Adrian, her son Khathfyre and her brother Seth. Juliet and I did the interview in the living room. During our conversation, I spoke about what brought me to Gambia, why repatriation to Africa is important, my thoughts on life in Gambia, and the legacy of former Zimbabwe president Robert Mugabe (who died the day before our interview). I also mentioned my book *The Rise of Rastafari: Resistance, Redemption & Repatriation*.

I decided to reschedule the date of Juliet's interview for my documentary because of a few reasons. One of those reasons was because I wanted to be better equipped with questions to ask her. A big issue was the weather conditions, it started to rain heavily and I didn't want the noise interference in the background from the rain. It was also getting dark outside and the camcorder I had wasn't very good at recording in low light conditions. At that point, we didn't have any video lights that we could use to improve the lighting in the room for recording.

After we finished my interview, Juliet and I started to talk more about what she would be doing on the Blaxit YouTube channel in the future. Juliet told me she was looking for a videographer and video editor for Blaxit. I told Juliet that I would suit doing that because of my experience in filming and editing videos. I have a degree in Sports Journalism. As part of my course, I regularly filmed videos, presented shows, did voiceovers, and edited videos. I also used to film and edit home videos as a hobby. In 2017, I worked on a project with BBC Three about Kwanzaa. The video I presented has had over 30,000 views on BBC Three's Facebook page.

The next day, I started my role as a freelance videographer and video editor for Blaxit. During the following week, I filmed and edited videos of people Juliet interviewed. Harona Drammeh (CEO of Paradise TV) was one of the people that was interviewed on Blaxit during that period. In Gambia, Harona is a renowned journalist and he has over 30 years' experience in the industry.

During my time working on Blaxit, I mingled with the *movers and shakers* of Gambia. I filmed and edited videos of high profile Gambians including Essa Faal (Lead Counsel of the Truth,

Reconciliation and Reparations Commission), Halifa Sallah (Minister of Parliament), Amadou Sanneh (Nephew of Gambia President Adama Barrow), E.N.C (one of the country's most popular music artists), "Fatty" Danso (Gambia national team footballer), Abubakar Bensouda (Blue Ocean Properties Managing Director), Saul Frazer (CEO of Global Properties), Jainaba Sonko (presenter on QTV), Tony Mendy and Isatu Bokum (EYEGAMBIA journalists), Tedla Khan (Partner and Managing Director of Azeb Capital LLC), Dembo Kambi (Chairman of the Gambia National Youth Council), and Ousman Bah (Chief Executive officer of IIHT Technology Institute).

Although Juliet and I didn't interview the following people on Blaxit, we did meet Hamat Bah (Minister of Tourism and leader of the National Reconciliation Party), Malick Kah (QTV General Manager), and Musa Sise (Africell Senior Public Relations and Media Manager). Juliet and I also met the brother of the Gambia President Adama Barrow. And, I recall meeting the director and management team of Trust Bank Limited. In addition to meeting the *who's who* of Gambia, Juliet and I also spent time with famous YouTube vloggers Dynast Amir and Dr. Mumbi Seraki. The renowned vloggers visited Gambia at separate times. During their time in Gambia, Dynast Amir stayed at Juliet's house.

Dr. Mumbi Seraki stayed at The Tranquil Star guest house, which is owned by Juliet's friend Christine and her husband Ron.

Every week, Juliet and I did videos with influential people. Every now and again, I used to watch the Gambian television channel QTV. When I watched the channel, I would often see someone on the TV that was on one of our Blaxit videos or someone that I had met before. At the Pan-African Youth Conference, we met a young university student called Ousman Touray. He told us that he's a Blaxit subscriber and that he had watched our previous videos on Blaxit (including my interview with Juliet).

After speaking with Ousman briefly, Juliet interviewed him and I filmed the interview. I uploaded Ousman's interview on Blaxit with the other video footage that I edited from The Pan African Youth Conference. From that video I uploaded, someone copied a short clip of Ousman's interview and shared it. The short clip of Ousman's interview went viral. I have seen that video clip shared on multiple platforms by people from different countries. The video has almost 500,000 views on the YouTube channel *Voice TV Nigeria*. It also has 38,000 views on the YouTube channel *Make Afrika Great*. The original video footage I filmed at The Pan African Youth Conference with Ousman's interview, has had over 39,000 views on the Blaxit YouTube channel.

At one point, I was seeing the video clip of Ousman in several places every day and this was even months after we uploaded the original video on YouTube. I was pleasantly surprised when I found out that Julius Malema, the leader of South Africa's Economic Freedom Fighters (EFF) political party, posted the video we did of Ousman on one of his social media pages. Malema commented on the video saying, "The future of our continent looks bright; the young must continue to be vigilant and focused." For someone as prestige as Julius Malema to post that video on his platform, shows how much of an impact that our Blaxit video of Ousman had across social media.

As a result of Ousman's interview on Blaxit, he has become famous worldwide and he has been going from strength to strength. Since that interview, Ousman has gained thousands of supporters, he has been helped with funds to study at the University of Rwanda, he has become an ambassador at the University of The Gambia, and he has been appointed as the Pan African Heritage World Youth Ambassador. Ousman has *won the hearts* of many fellow Africans by rejecting scholarship opportunities to study in the West, so that he would remain in

Africa and go to study at the University of Rwanda. In his interview on Blaxit, Ousman said: "No one is going to do it for us (Africans), if we our all running away, when are we going to make it? We have to stay in Africa, develop in Africa, and then show to the world that Africa has a better image than the one they portray in the West."

In our first three months, Blaxit gained over 20,000 subscribers. Our average amount of viewers per video was over 10,000 views. Blaxit was being watched globally. The majority of our viewers were from the USA. We also had a large amount of our viewers from the UK. Blaxit subscribers were sending us videos about their experiences and thoughts of living in the West. Some of them had lived in Africa before, some of them were planning to move to Gambia. I edited and uploaded the videos sent to us by the Blaxit subscribers. Juliet decided to name those type of videos, *Blaxit Messengers*.

As a result of our popular videos on YouTube, a lot of Blaxit subscribers came to Gambia to experience *the smiling coast of Africa*. There was an influx of Blaxit subscribers coming to Gambia on a weekly basis. Due to the popularity of Blaxit, we hosted the Blaxit Link Up. This was an informal gathering every Sunday that we organised so we could spend time with our subscribers that had come to Gambia. We held these gatherings at Solomon's Beach Bar & Restaurant by Palma Rima Beach.

During the Blaxit Link Up, I filmed interviews with Juliet speaking to Blaxit subscribers about their experience and thoughts of their time spent in Gambia. On Sundays, a lot of people go to Palm Rima Beach to socialise, relax in the hot weather, or to take part in different activities on the beach. It's common to see young males playing sport such as football or wrestling. I remember on one occasion when we were at the beach, Juliet's son got on a horse and went on a ride with the horse driver.

I decided to hold back from doing my documentary and instead focused on my work with Blaxit. My first reason for this was because I didn't want to replicate the same kind of work that I had already done with Blaxit. My second reason was because it made sense to focus on the Blaxit videos as I was getting paid for doing them. My third reason was because I thought my documentary would have reached a very small audience compared to the amount of people who were watching Blaxit. And, my final reason was because I wouldn't have had enough time to work on Blaxit and do my documentary.

The main purpose of the Blaxit YouTube channel is to encourage people of African heritage living in the diaspora to move to Africa (particularly Gambia) and to encourage those from the diaspora to help develop *the smiling coast of Africa* by investing in the Gambia (e.g. setting up business, buying land, helping with the infrastructure, and supporting the Gambian economy financially). To attract people to come to *the smiling coast of Africa*, Juliet and I showcased the best parts of Gambia on Blaxit and we tried to present media that would make people look at Gambia in a positive way. We wanted to counteract the negative portrayal that is shown of African countries in Western media.

Negative propaganda about Africa is put out purposely to suit the interest of Western powers. They have created a stigma against Africa to discourage black people from going back to Africa and helping Africa develop. Western powers want to continue to capitalise on Africa and exploit Africa for its resources, so that these Western beneficiaries can make money to develop the West and they can maintain the status quo. They don't want black people in the diaspora taking their money from the West to Africa. Western governments are run by remorseless white supremacists who will do everything they can do to stop Africa prospering. It is their intention to keep a division between black people in the West and black people on the African continent.

Many people in Africa grow up thinking that *the streets of Europe are paved with gold*. In search of what they believe will be a better life, they try to move to Europe. Whilst there are opportunities in European countries, there are also risks and disadvantages too. Some Africans try to come to Europe through *the backway* by getting on a boat and crossing the country border illegally. People who do that, risk their lives in this process.

Many people who try to go to Europe through *the backway*, do not make it and they die along the journey. You have others who fall victim to human traffickers and they become enslaved. For those who manage to get to Europe *through the backway*, a lot of them find themselves in difficulties and in worser situations than they were back in the countries they came from. On December 4, 2019, at least 62 Gambians died on one journey trying to get to Europe *the backway* via boat. I know someone who lost a few of his family members because they were on the boat that sunk.

Independent journalists and content creators of the 21st century have more control on the media than ever before! Nowadays, traditional mainstream news corporations are becoming less powerful because of competition. There are so many media platforms that are providing a wide variety of content to the public. Modern technology means that anyone can be a content creator by posting a video from their phone or by taking a picture and sharing it on social media.

The internet allows people to access media at their fingertips. Platforms such as YouTube have countless number of videos that provide news and information about all kinds of things. Social media platforms such as Facebook, WhatApp, and Instagram allow people to come across a constant influx of posts containing news and information on different topics. As a result of this, people are able to access more information from different perspectives than what they would have previously been exposed to.

People acquiring more information from different sources helps people to verify and evaluate things. Hence, people can come to better conclusions and make better judgements than they did in the past when there was limited access to information and often the information presented was bias in order to push a certain narrative. Today's social media is very powerful because content creators have international platforms where they can spread their media work and reach large audiences. An ordinary person can become famous overnight and information can be spread rapidly across the world. Social media platforms also help people build a following.

Juliet and I used the Blaxit YouTube channel as our vehicle of delivering our own narrative and providing content to inspire our people about moving to Africa (particularly Gambia). During my time working with Juliet on Blaxit, we filmed and uploaded videos on YouTube of people from the diaspora who had moved to Gambia. This gave our audience an insight into the journey of those *African returnees*. We also produced videos that showcased Gambian-owned businesses, places of interest, and people of influence in Gambia.

Juliet and I did a wide variety of videos. Earlier in this chapter, I mentioned some of the people we interviewed for Blaxit. Below is a list of some of the other videos we uploaded on Blaxit:

- A guide to buying land in Gambia.
- An interview with an estate agent.
- An interview with a senior police officer.
- A tour of a medical centre.
- A visit to the local supermarket.
- The naming ceremony of Gambia president Adama Barrow's brother.

- A tour of Hyperlink hotel.
- A day out at Makasutu Culture Forest.
- The African Youth Leadership Awards.
- An interview with the owner of African Queen Restaurant.
- An interview with the owner of Mosiah's Jamaican Bar and Restaurant.
- A dinner with Dynast Amir.
- Highlights of my lecture that I delivered about Rastafari to the students at Brusubi Upper and Senior Secondary School.
- Juliet's speech to students at the University of The Gambia.
- A video of King Baker Bakery featuring the Co-Owner Ousman Demba.

One day, Juliet and I went into one of the local schools. The children were so happy to see us. They came up to us, shook our hands, held onto us, and they were cheering us on. When we went into the school and was leaving, they gave us a reception as if we were royalty or celebrities. The children at this school didn't have modern equipment or resources like children in England have. But those Gambian children were so happy. I have never seen school children in England as happy as how those Gambian children were. At one of the schools we visited, we managed to help them get computers that had been donated from one of our Blaxit subscribers.

Juliet and I have played a key role in facilitating the move of black people from the diaspora to Gambia. The Gambian economy and the native people in Gambia are benefiting from the investments and developments of *African returnees*. As a result of the work Juliet and I have done on Blaxit and the relationships we have had with our subscribers, so many people have bought land in Gambia, have moved to Gambia, or they have plans to relocate to Gambia in the future.

Juliet and I were more than just YouTube vloggers trying to get views on our channel. We were unofficial ambassadors of Gambia. We met up with our Blaxit subscribers, hosted them, showed them around Gambia, and helped them with whatever they needed from us (within our means). Some of our Blaxit subscribers wanted general advice about Gambia before coming over, some wanted help or advice about buying land, some wanted business advice, and some just wanted to spend time with us.

I am proud of being a pioneer in the influx of black people from the diaspora who have decided to *Blaxit* to *the Motherland*. There are many people who had never heard of Gambia or didn't know where Gambia was on the map until they watched our Blaxit videos. Some of these people are now living in Gambia. That goes to show how much of a strong impact that Blaxit has made.

Before Blaxit, Gambia wasn't a destination most black people in the diaspora talked about when speaking about Africa. But since then, Gambia (the smallest country in mainland Africa) has become one of the most popular African destinations for people to travel to and/or talk about. Blaxit has changed so many people's lives because the Blaxit videos have inspired people to move to Gambia (Africa) and these people are living a better quality of life in Gambia compared to how they lived in the West.

Blaxit was the catalyst to many other YouTube channels that were created later on by other vloggers from the diaspora who have gone to Gambia and also decided to focus on making content about Gambia on their YouTube channel. When Blaxit launched, there wasn't other YouTube channels that were showcasing regular content about Gambia in the way how Blaxit was doing it. As Blaxit became very popular, other YouTubers from the diaspora followed pursuit by also vlogging about Gambia.

I salute Juliet and her husband Adrian for their continuous devotion in helping people of

African heritage from the diaspora with moving and settling in *the smiling coast of Africa*. Juliet and Adrian are genuine and trustworthy people, who are committed to bringing black people together and developing Gambia. During my time at Blaxit, I spent so much time with Juliet and Adrian that it was almost as if I was part of their family. I used to be with them every day. Most days, I would be at their house till early hours of the morning doing the video editing and uploading the latest Blaxit video. It was like I was *part of the furniture* at their house.

CHAPTER 11

On 22 September, 2019, Thomas Cook went bust. This was just weeks before the start of the upcoming tourist season. Thomas Cook had been flying to Gambia for decades. Before it went bust, Thomas Cook used to operate regular flights to Gambia every week during tourist season. Hence, Thomas Cook was the most frequently used airline for people in England travelling to Gambia during that time of year. English tourists travelling via Thomas Cook made up a large amount of the number of tourists visiting Gambia.

Tourism is one of the industries that makes the most money for the Gambian economy. In Gambia, many people live *hand to mouth* and struggle to *make ends meet* even during the *usual* tourist season. Due to Thomas Cook's demise, all flights to Gambia by Thomas Cook were stopped; this caused a big decline of the country's tourism industry. Hotels, bars, clubs, restaurants, local street vendors, taxi drivers, and retail shops were hit hard. Most of those businesses experienced a big reduction in their number of customers and sales compared to previous years.

Midway through December, I remember having a conversation with my friend Bounty. We were speaking about the effect of Thomas Cook going out of business on the tourism industry in Gambia. Bounty told me that Badala Park Hotel hadn't even reached a quarter of its capacity. The previous year when I stayed at Badala Park Hotel during the same month of December, the hotel was almost fully booked.

My friend Sailou relies heavily on tourist customers for his shop. Therefore, his business was struggling with the effect of Thomas Cook no longer flying tourists to Gambia. There were still some English people who had travelled via an alternative airline and there were tourists from other countries. However, there were significantly fewer tourists than usual at that time of year. Sailou told me that the English tourists are the ones who tend to buy more from him and that they also spend more money at his shop than tourists from other countries.

When I visited Gambia during February, 2019 (my second time in Gambia), there was a specific tourist taxi driver that I used a few times during the week I stayed in Gambia. Towards the end of my third time in Gambia (December 2019), I saw that same taxi driver that I used earlier that year in February. I was walking in Senegambia and he was on the side of the road. When I saw him, it was approaching evening time and he hadn't eaten since the previous day.

The tourist taxi driver was in need of money to get some food to eat. He normally makes his money through taxi jobs from tourist customers that he usually gets at that time of the year. But on this occasion, he had no money because he wasn't getting jobs from tourist customers. This was due to less tourists in Gambia because of Thomas Cook going out of business.

During the third time I was in Gambia, the government were in the process of drafting a new constitution. Descendants of the enslaved Africans who were taken from Gambia and other places in West Africa, want more than a verbal "Welcome home" from our brothers and sisters living in Gambia (this also applies to whatever African country we are returning to). We also want citizenship, so we are legally recognised as Gambian/African and given a permanent right to stay in the country, with the same rights and laws that apply to natives born in Gambia (or whatever African country we chose to reside in).

Our ancestors that were enslaved never left Africa by their own free will; they were kidnapped and forcefully taken from Africa. Before Africa was colonised by Europeans, there were no borders separating these places like there are now. Africans had been travelling throughout Africa for thousands of years without boarder restrictions. Africa used to be a landmass made up of different tribes and kingdoms. When Africa was colonised by Europeans during the scramble for Africa, Europeans divided Africa into countries and created boarders between countries.

Immigration and boarder control laws created by colonisers are still in place in the majority of African countries. This means that descendants of enslaved Africans returning back home to Africa, are not recognised as Africans by law. When entering an African country (including Gambia), descendants of enslaved Africans have to follow the same immigration laws as white or Asian people that live outside of Africa, even though those people don't have the same connection to Africa as descendants of enslaved Africans do.

In Gambia, the law states that you have to

wait fifteen years before you can acquire citizenship in that country if you're a foreigner (non-Gambian citizen) or you must be married to a Gambian for seven years before you can apply for citizenship. If you want to live in Gambia long-term and you aren't a Gambian citizen, you must get a residence permit and renew your residence permit every year. There are fee's you must pay every year to renew your residency. To add insult, when you get your residence permit, you are given an ID card which is officially called an *alien card*.

When I was in Gambia, they were in the process of redrafting a new constitution. *African returnees* living in Gambia recommended a clause that would give automatic citizenship to descendants of enslaved Africans who have relocated from the diaspora to Gambia. The campaign for automatic citizenship was primarily led by members of the Diaspora Returnee Association and Juliet Ryan from Blaxit. There was another recommendation, which was to add a clause to the draft constitution that would give *African returnees* the same rights as native Gambians when buying land, selling land, and passing on land to family as inheritance.

On 16 December, 2019, there was a public consultation which was held by the Gambian

Constitutional Review Committee (CRC). That event was attended by members of Blaxit (including myself). It was also attended by the Diaspora Returnee Association and several other *African returnees* who live in Gambia. During the CRC public consultation, there were speeches from *African returnees* who presented their case in support of automatic citizenship and land rights for *African returnees*. A petition with letters from *African returnees* and people of African heritage in the diaspora was given to the facilitator of the CRC public consultation. The letters were in support of the automatic citizenship campaign.

CHAPTER 12

At the beginning of December (2019), I decided that I was going to go back to England later that month. I went to The Gambia Experience office in Senegambia and booked my flight ticket. I made the decision to go back to England so that I could save up money to travel and experience another country in Africa. One of the reasons why I left Gambia after six months, was because I couldn't see long-term financial stability for me if I stayed in Gambia.

I enjoyed the work I was doing with Blaxit. But I would have needed more money than I was getting paid to sustain my living costs in the long-run. In Gambia, I saw very little career opportunities or viable businesses in my areas of expertise, whether that be through self-employment or employment. Gambia is not the most suitable place to be if you are a young person starting or developing a career. Gambia is more suitable for people who already have substantial amounts of money to set up a business or for those who already have streams of income to sustain their living costs (this could be from return on investments, property rent, a pension, or an existing business). Gambia is not somewhere you will go from *rags to riches* by relying on money made in Gambia. This is because the country's economy is very weak. Therefore, most Gambians either go abroad or want to go abroad to make money.

Many Gambians who go abroad, comeback to Gambia and are in a better financial situation because of the money they acquired whilst working abroad. When these Gambians return to settle in Gambia, they utilise the skills that they had learned abroad and set up businesses in their area of expertise. This helps with employment and development in Gambia. Money that *returning Gambians* bring into the country benefits the economy because its money being spent in Gambia.

Although Gambians in the diaspora who come home are doing great things, Gambia needs to be more self-sufficient. There must be more opportunities for its citizens, so the people can stay in Gambia and prosper in their own country instead of having to go to the West to acquire wealth and skills to comeback to Gambia. The Gambian economy also needs to be in a stronger position, so fewer of its citizens need to rely on remittance money from relatives, partners, and friends who are abroad.

A big problem is that Gambia relies so much on tourism. Thomas Cook going out of business and no longer operating flights to Gambia, was a perfect example of how bad things can be for some of the locals if the tourism industry is disrupted. Another problem with the Gambian economy relying on tourism, is that Gambia will continue to be at the mercy of foreign governments, foreign travel companies, foreign business owners, and foreign tourists.

Whilst moving to Gambia may not be the best long-term option if you don't have much money or existing streams of income, Gambia is an amazing place with wonderful people and I would definitely recommend that people at least go Gambia on holiday and experience *the smiling coast of Africa*. Gambia exceeded my expectations on each of the three times I went there. I had the *time of my life* every time I went Gambia. All three of my trips to Gambia were special to me in their own way. I have so much fond memories from being in Gambia and I am still in contact with lots of my friends that I made when I was over there.

In my last two weeks before I left, I took a break from working with Blaxit and spent some quality time with my Gambian friends. I also spent time with my friends Joseph (Founder and CEO of Joe Ride - a transportation company in Gambia) and Hughie Rose (Founder and CEO of AGA Tours - a company that operates tours in Gambia). Joseph and Hughie live in England but they operate businesses in Gambia.

I had spoken to Joseph on the phone before I went to Gambia. However, I hadn't met him in person before going to Gambia. Joseph and I got on really well as soon as we met. I was put in contact with Joseph by Dr. Aboo. Joseph and I went to some bars and clubs. Joseph was staying in Gambia for a week at one of the hotels on the popular Senegambia strip. I had met Hughie just once before I came to Gambia. We were both at an event held by Luton Black Men Community Group. During my time in Gambia, I got to know Hughie much better.

Ironically, I spent more time with many people that I know or know of from England whilst I was in Gambia compared to the amount of time I had spent with these people whilst in England. There was a community of like-minded *conscious black* people in Gambia. These were mainly black people that had come from

England or USA, who ether lived in Gambia or were visiting Gambia. Therefore, I had people who I could relate to that were coming from a similar background and mindset as me. I also had lots of friends who were either native Gambians or residents in Gambia from other African countries. My social life in Gambia was great. I also really valued the bonds I made with my regular taxi drivers, who I became friends with.

On my penultimate evening in Gambia, I spent time downstairs from my flat at the mini mart with Assan, Njie and one of my friends from the car park. I remember that night being a little bit chilly, so I put on one of my tracksuit tops. It was one of the few times during my six months stay in Gambia that I wore something on top of my t-shirt to keep me warm. During the evenings, sometimes the temperature would drop. When that happened, the weather would usually still remain at a warm temperature. But on this particular evening, it was different.

I remember being in the mini mart and then suddenly starting to feel very cold. Then, I began shivering. I asked the others about whether they felt cold. Even though they were wearing less layers of clothing than me, none of them felt cold. So, I knew this wasn't to do with the weather and that I was unwell. I thought I had got malaria, so I went upstairs to my room and took two malaria tablets with water. I fell asleep shortly after taking the tablets.

When I got up the next morning, I felt fine. But as a precaution, I decided to go to the medical centre to get tested for malaria. While I was at the medical centre, I decided to get a full check up to see if I was in good health (especially because I was going back to England the next day). From the results I got back, it confirmed I didn't have malaria or any other diseases. My health was in good condition. I do know people from England who have caught malaria in Gambia. Fortunately, they have been cured after going to hospital and receiving the right treatment.

Malaria is one of the most dangerous diseases in the world. It causes hundreds of thousands of deaths around the world every year. Malaria is prominent in Sub-Sahara Africa and parts of Asia (especially India). There are tablets you can take for malaria but you may experience bad side effects. Some people use natural remedies to prevent malaria, including the use of moringa. One of the most common natural ways people prevent malaria, is by drinking herbal tea made by mixing moringa leaves and water (drunk on a daily basis). Alternatively, people can take one moringa seed a day.

Most local Gambians don't use any treatment to prevent malaria. It has become like catching the flu to them (something that happens every once in a while, within a few years). Malaria is a lot more dangerous than the flu, especially if malaria is not treated within a certain amount of time. If you are going to Gambia, I would recommend you buy mosquito repellent and apply it to your skin to protect yourself from malaria. The best mosquito repellent I used was called Odomos.

Malaria can spread very quickly and the symptoms can be very bad. The symptoms include shivering, feeling cold when it's hot, diarrhoea, fever, headache, nausea, vomiting, and abdominal pain. If you get malaria, there are medications and hospital treatment which can cure you from the disease. If you start to develop malaria symptoms, you should get this checked out as soon as possible. Malaria can kill you if it's not treated in time. If you don't have quick access to a doctor to get medical support, you may find that taking malaria tablets may help to relieve your symptoms. Even if you start to feel better after taking the tablets, it's best to get checked by a doctor as soon as possible *to be on the safe side*.

Malaria is caused by getting bitten by an

infected female mosquito. Extra precaution should be taken between dusk and dawn and near areas where there is large standing water. You can get malaria tablets in pharmacies across Gambia. They will normally have an expensive brand of malaria tablets and a cheaper brand of malaria tablets. Either of them can be used to prevent malaria. There are more mosquitos around during the rainy season compared to during the dry season.

On 23 December, 2019, I went back to England. That day was very emotional for me. I felt sad about going back to England and leaving everyone in Gambia. I knew I was going to miss everyone and miss living in Gambia. When I left Gambia, I felt like I was leaving my country. In my heart, I wanted to remain in Gambia. But my mind was telling me to go back to England and save up some more money, so I would be in a better position to explore more options and make a permanent move to Africa in the future.

When I got back to England, I was treated like a criminal as soon as I got to the airport. When I was passing through immigration, I was stopped and searched by the police officer for drugs. The policeman interrogated me about what I was doing abroad in Gambia. He kept asking me about whether I had been dealing drugs. The policeman also asked me questions about what country I was born in and where I got my suitcase from. The policeman took my passport to check if I had a criminal record. He scanned my suitcase through the machine to check that I wasn't smuggling drugs in my suitcase. At that point I thought to myself, I had gone from being treated like *royalty* in Gambia to being treated like a *criminal* in England. That incident with the police officer, reinforced my view that I don't belong in England and how much of a racist country England is. In a nutshell, it summed up exactly what's wrong with England!

I stayed with my mum for the first few days I was back in England. After that, I went to stay with my friend in Leighton Buzzard. During my first few weeks back in England, I felt like a foreigner in a strange country. After being in a black country for a lengthy period of time, it seemed odd and like a culture shock when I got back to England and saw so many white people. It took a few weeks for me to get refamiliarised with seeing lots of white people around when I was going out.

Gambia was definitely a more conducive environment for me to be in. I felt a sense of belonging in Gambia. I was in an environment in which I was free to express myself as a black person, without having to endure the day-to-day pressures of being a black man in a country like England that treats black people like second class citizens. It's a shame that I had to go to another country outside of the country I was born in, in order to experience what it is like to be treated like a normal person in a society where I am fully embraced. I wasn't black or brown in Gambia, I was a human being.

ABOUT THE AUTHOR

Makonnen Sankofa is a best-selling author, entrepreneur, radio presenter, public speaker, journalist, and community activist. Makonnen was born and raised in England. His ethnicity is African-Caribbean. Makonnen and his brother were raised in a single mother household in South East London. But Makonnen left home to go to study at Southampton Solent University when he was 19. During his time living in Southampton, he gained broader knowledge and experience of life.

Although Makonnen adapted to life in Southampton and was popular at University, being in Southampton initially was a big culture shock to him. During his time in Southampton, Makonnen began questioning racial inequalities that he saw happening around him and in the world. This gradually led Makonnen into the direction of black consciousness. Makonnen became inspired by the Rastafari Movement and also by black activists such as Mutabaruka, Malcolm X, Marcus Garvey, Amos Wilson, Umar Johnson, Robert Mugabe, Ray Hagins, Claude Anderson, Brother Leader Mbandaka, Khalid Muhammad, and Louis Farrakhan.

Makonnen stayed in Southampton for four years. He studied Sports Journalism for two years before he put his studies on hold in his final year, due to mental health issues. During his break from studying Sports Journalism, Makonnen set up a business. He began selling official football merchandise. The products he sold included photographs, posters, clothing, drinking glasses, headwear, footballs, bedding, stationary, mugs, calendars, backpacks, gym bags, teddy bears, holdalls, mobile phone cases, keyrings, and confectionary.

Makonnen's football merchandise business was called The Football Shop. He started off by trading at the Marlands Shopping Centre in Southampton. He traded there for four months before he decided to move the business to Luton Indoor Market. The Football Shop was in business at Luton Indoor Market for 1 year before the business ceased trading. After the demise of Makonnen's football merchandise business, he finished his final year of Sports Journalism at the University of Bedfordshire (Luton campus). He later went on to establish himself in the sales industry. Makonnen already had experience from working in sales because he had sales jobs during his time studying in Southampton. He has gone from strength to strength in sales, becoming a top salesman for some of the most established companies globally and nationally.

Makonnen preferred living in Luton to Southampton because there is a large black community in Luton. He was a member of the Luton Black Men Community Group until it dissolved in 2020. One of the aims of the group, was to provide solutions to issues affecting black communities. Another aim of the Luton Black Men Community Group, was to help those in the group improve their leadership skills. Luton Black Men Community Group hosted a wide variety of events throughout the year. Makonnen has also been involved in groups such as the African Heritage Network of Luton and the interim National Afrikan People's Parliament. He has spent the best part of a decade as a community activist.

Makonnen founded The Black Books Webinar in May 2020. The event is also hosted by Makonnen. Each month, he invites different authors of African heritage to come on his webinar and speak about their books. The Black Book Webinar showcases the wide variety of books written by authors of African heritage. These books include genres such as children's books, history, relationships, culture, health, poetry, and real-life stories.

Makonnen is the best-selling author of *The Rise of Rastafari: Resistance, Redemption & Repatriation*. He released that as his debut book in May 2019. Makonnen wrote *The Rise of Rastafari* to dispel the common misconceptions people have of Rastafari and to highlight the core principles of Rastafari such as nation building, repatriation to Africa, resistance to white supremacy, and Pan-Africanism. *The Rise of Rastafari* also gives key in-depth knowledge about the origins of Rastafari, which is often untold.

Makonnen is a big advocate of repatriation to Africa for black people living in the diaspora. At the time of writing this book, Makonnen is in the process of arranging to move to Zambia (South East Africa).

CONNECT WITH AUTHOR MAKONEN SANKOFA

If you enjoyed reading this book *Life in Gambia: The Smiling Coast of Africa*, please leave a review on Amazon and recommend the book to your friends, relatives, and people you know. You can leave a review on Amazon regardless of where you bought the book.

Email: makonnensankofa@hotmail.com

Facebook: Makonnen Sankofa

Instagram: @makonnen.sankofa

YouTube channel: Makonnen Sankofa

RESISTANCE, REDEMPTION & REPATRIATION

Makonnen Sankofa

The Rise of Rastafari:
Resistance, Redemption &
Repatriation

Makonnen Sankofa

Available on Amazon
in
Paperback and Kindle

5.0 out of 5 stars
A "must have" guide to understanding Rastafarianism
Reviewed in the United Kingdom on 23 November 2019
Verified Purchase

A truly fascinating book which can be picked up and read by absolutely anybody. The writer's conversational and easy-going style ensures that all readers will be gripped by this much misunderstood topic. A good, clear user-friendly guide which is essential reading for anyone who wants a clear explanation of the essential meaning of Rastafarianism.

5.0 out of 5 stars
RASTA MUST READ!!!
Reviewed in the United Kingdom on 4 August 2020
Verified Purchase

This book is the only book that has broken down & explained all the misconceptions & notions about Rastafari & Rastafarianism for everyone to read. To this day there are many common untruths which people still hold on to but this book goes into great detail to set them straight. Stamp of Approval on my path!!

5.0 out of 5 stars
An interesting read about Rastafarianism
Reviewed in the United Kingdom on 6 March 2020

This book discusses the origins of Rastafarianism and pan activism in a straightforward an informative manner, dispelling myths about Rastafarians along the way. I would definitely recommend this book to young adults at schools, colleges and universities. An excellent well researched read.